101
SNAPPY
SERMONETTES

for the children's church

PAUL E. HOLDCRAFT

ABINGDON PRESS

New York • *Nashville*

To

Calvin
David
Richard
Elaine
Susan

FOREWORD

THIS book is designed to help busy pastors, church workers, and Christian parents with their regular or occasional responsibility of giving talks to children.

The "Children's Church" idea is gaining momentum. Everywhere congregations able to do so are fitting up chapels, or worship centers, especially for children, where services are conducted for them during the usual church worship period. If adequate leadership is available, this separate service has very great value.

Not having the trained leadership and equipment, many pastors find an alternate plan very satisfactory. This plan calls for a five-minute sermonette to the children as a part of the regular church service. By taking the five minutes from the main sermon, the service is not lengthened. Usually the sermonette is given after the liturgical part of the service. For the sermonette some pastors prefer to come down from the pulpit and stand closer to the children, who should occupy the front seats. After the sermonette a hymn is sung and the children may retire, or go to the seats occupied by their parents.

Any church, no matter how small, may without additional equipment or leadership follow this plan. Pastors who have tried it have been amazed by the evident appreciation of not only the children, but the adults as well. The parents not only appreciate what the pastor is trying to do for their children but seem to get personal inspiration from the sermonettes. Indeed, one pastor confesses that he gets more compliments on his sermonettes than on his sermons.

A wise old bishop, addressing a class of young ministers, gave this bit of advice: "When you preach, pick out a child in the audience and make your message so simple the child can understand it, and let the rest of the people shift for themselves." This is good advice.

If Jesus felt it was worth while to stop talking with adults and give some of his time to the little children, perhaps we too may discover that the children should have at least five minutes out of an adult-centered worship service.

P. E. H.

CONTENTS

YOU CAN'T FOOL GOD

A FATHER once gave his young son a letter to be mailed. "Here," he said, "take this to the corner drugstore, buy a stamp and put it on the envelope, then drop it in the mailbox." When the little boy came home, he was as happy as could be. "Father," he said, "I saved the three cents. I saw a lot of people dropping letters in the mailbox, and I waited until no one was in sight, then I dropped our letter in without having to buy a stamp." He really thought he had done something smart. Of course Daddy had to explain to the boy what a mistake he had made. He said, "You can't fool Uncle Sam. The letter will either come back for postage, or the person to receive it will have to pay the postage, and it is even possible the letter may wind up in the dead letter office. You just can't fool Uncle Sam that easy."

A lot of people—not only children—think they can fool God. They desecrate God's holy Sabbath day, pay no heed to the call of the church bells, neglect their Bibles and prayer, and they think it makes no difference. They think God pays no attention to their neglect. The little boy in the story really thought he was getting by without paying for the stamp, and a lot of people think they are getting by without making much of an investment in the church. The little boy thought Uncle Sam ought to take that letter without being paid the price of the stamp. And a lot of people think God ought to give them all the benefits and blessings of religion, and of the church, without any expense or effort on their part.

The little boy went through all the motions of mailing a letter, and he probably thought everything was all right. But Uncle Sam didn't think so. Some people profess to be very religious, but they really are not. Jesus called such people hypocrites. He admitted that outwardly they appeared to be very sincere, but as he looked into their hearts,

9

he saw they were just trying to fool God and get by without doing God's will.

THE PAY FOR PROFANITY

SEVERAL YOUNG fellows were conversing with each other at a party and one of them insisted upon using a great deal of profanity, or as we often say, "cuss words." Another of the young men was a Christian, and after a while he mildly asked the profane youth, "Who pays you to swear?" "Why, nobody," he promptly replied. "Well," said the Christian youth, "you surely work cheap—to sacrifice the character of a gentleman, to offend your friends, to disgrace the good name of your family, and risk the wrath of God. You surely work cheap." The profane boy didn't know the answer to that one.

Here is a good definition of profanity you may wish to use some time: "Profanity is the effort of a feeble mind to express itself forcibly."

A minister used to carry with him a supply of cards on which a little verse was printed. Whenever he heard someone say a bad word, or take God's name in vain, he would smilingly present the offender with a card. Here is the verse, written by William Cowper:

> It chills my blood to hear the blest Supreme
> Rudely appealed to on each trifling theme;
> Maintain your rank, vulgarity despise;
> To swear is neither brave, polite, nor wise.
> You would not swear upon the bed of death:
> Reflect! Your Maker yet may stop your breath.

It has been said, "A swearing parrot doesn't reason; that's why he swears." If he had reasoning powers, he wouldn't say bad words. One has to wonder if a lot of people, old and young, whom we hear saying profane words really have reasoning powers.

Memory Verse

"Thou shalt not take the name of the Lord thy God in vain."—Exod. 20:7

A THOUGHT OF MOTHER
(MOTHER'S DAY)

MANY YEARS ago a boy in his early teens was in a boat about a mile from land. Suddenly a storm came up, and before the boy could get back to the shore, the strong wind and high waves upset the boat, throwing him into the water. Now the boy was a good swimmer, and so he swam bravely toward the shore. His mother and others were on the shore watching, and praying, and in great distress.

More than once the high waves went over him and he seemed to be lost. Friends set out in a lifeboat, but they could make little headway against the storm. It seemed that the boy's strength was giving out and all on the shore were sure he was about to drown. Then all of a sudden he seemed to get new strength and he renewed his battle with the waves. Finally he was dragged out on the shore, exhausted but very much alive.

After he had rested, someone asked him about the sudden strength that came to him that saved his life. He answered, "I thought of my mother." As it seemed certain he would drown, he thought of his widowed mother—how great would be her grief; he thought of his mother's need of him to help support the family. The very thought of his mother gave him new strength and courage and it was that sudden spurt of strength that saved his life. That boy later became the governor of the great state of Massachusetts.

A loving thought of mother has saved many a boy and girl from death, and from things worse than death. A thought of mother has saved many a young person from a life of sin and shame. Many thousands of those who are behind prison bars, or in drunkards' graves, or who are suffering from terrible diseases might have saved all their sufferings and troubles by loving thoughts of mother.

Boys and girls, when you are tempted to do wrong, whatever the wrong may be, just think of your mother—how it would break her heart and make her suffer. The mere thought of a good mother will help keep you strong and pure.

Memory Verse

"Honour thy father and thy mother: that thy days may be long upon the land which the Lord thy God giveth thee."—Exod. 20:12

TELL THE TRUTH

ABRAHAM LINCOLN was nicknamed "Honest Abe" because of his strict honesty. Time and again he had chances to do things whereby he would profit, but because they didn't seem honest to him, he refused to do them. Perhaps "Truthful George" would be a good nickname for George Washington. One of the stories about George as a boy is dear to the hearts of all Americans, the story of his cutting down a cherry tree, then refusing to tell a lie to try to avoid punishment. Someone has said, "A lie is a coward's way of getting out of trouble." The fact is that a lie usually gets you into more trouble than it can get you out of.

Now let us hear an old Persian legend of a boy named Selim. Selim was a camel driver, and one day his caravan was overtaken by robbers who took everybody's money and jewels and other valuables. When they came to Selim and searched his pockets, they could find no money. The robber chief then asked Selim, "Are you hiding any money?" Selim replied, "I have three gold pieces sewed up in a corner of my coat." "Why did you tell me?" asked the chief. Selim said, "Because my mother taught me three things—to be kind to everybody, to pray to God every day, and always to tell the truth."

This was something really new to the robber chief, to have a person tell him the truth when it meant the loss of his money. He thought for a moment, then said to Selim: "Here, instead of taking your three gold pieces, I am going to give you three. If I had had a mother like yours I wouldn't be a robber."

It may be expensive at times to tell the truth, and sometimes it is embarrassing, but it is always best in the end. Instead of a lie being a way out of trouble, it is a quick way into trouble. Nobody loves or respects a liar. In Proverbs we read that one of the things God hates is "a lying tongue." So let us always tell the truth. If it doesn't pay off in any other way, it will by giving us the satisfaction and peace of a good conscience.

Memory Verse

"Thou shalt not bear false witness against thy neighbour."—Exod. 20:16

SOME POTATOES

WHEN SOMEONE invents a new mechanical gadget, he may have it patented, which means no one else may infringe upon his rights. The inventor owns his idea. When someone writes a book, or a poem, he may have it copyrighted so no other person may make money out of it. When a person buys a house, or an automobile, he gets a title to it. Well, it is something like that with this world. "In the beginning God created the heaven and the earth." God created the universe; therefore it belongs to him. He owns it. He never gave it away, or sold it; therefore he still owns it. And if he still owns it, he has a just right to say what is to be done with it.

God has appointed man as his steward to look after his interests and manage his property. Now the Bible teaches us that God has told man he may have for his own use nine tenths of what he raises on the farms, or earns at his toil, but one tenth is God's and should be given for God's work.

Let us see how it works. Here are ten nice potatoes, all about the same size. Nine belong to man. They make quite a nice pile, do they not? But one potato is to be set aside for Christian work. Some people are so greedy and selfish that they won't give God the one potato, so they cut it in half and give him half of it. And I am afraid that some don't even give him a half. They give a fourth, or even less than that.

When God is so good to us that he gives us nine potatoes, should we not give him at least the one potato—the tithe—that he wants reserved for his work? And what goes for potatoes, goes also for apples, and onions, and parsnips, and corn. It also goes for the dollars and cents we may earn as wages at the mill or the office.

Someone has changed the words of a familiar verse of Scripture to make it read like this, "Begin now to tithe in the days of thy youth, while the stingy days come not . . . when thou shalt say, 'I have no pleasure in it.'"

Memory Verse

"All the tithe of the land . . . is the Lord's."—Lev. 27:30

A TWO-FACED MAN

FIVE HUNDRED years ago there lived in Italy a famous artist whose name was Leonardo da Vinci. Very few men in all the history of the world have had as many wonderful talents and could do so many different things, and do them well, as this great man. He was a poet, a sculptor, an architect, a philosopher, a musician, a scientist, and a machinist. He didn't just dabble in these things; he was a master in them all.

Perhaps the greatest achievement of Leonardo da Vinci was his masterpiece of art, "The Last Supper," which he painted on the wall of a convent. A story has come down through the years about this painting. It may not be true, but it could be true.

It seems the artist wanted first of all to paint the central figure, which was Christ. He looked far and wide for a young man to model for the picture. After months of searching he found a young man who sang in the choir of a church in Milan. His name was Pedro Bandandello. Pedro was a young man, very handsome in appearance; his features were mild and gentle, intelligence and culture marked his personality, and it was evident that he was a sincere Christian. So for months Pedro stood before the artist as a model for Christ. The years passed by, and the artist painted all the figures except Judas, the treacherous hypocrite and thief. Then the artist began his search for someone to model for Judas. Finally he found a dissipated man in a low tavern. He had been in all kinds of trouble with the law and was an outcast. When offered money to pose for the Judas picture, he was glad for the chance. Months passed by, and after the picture was completed, and not until then, the artist discovered that Pedro Bandandello was the same man who posed for both Christ and Judas. After posing as Jesus, he began a life of sin and drunkenness. Eight years passed before the artist needed a model for Judas, and in the meanwhile Pedro's appearance had so changed that he fitted that description too.

No matter how handsome and innocent one may be, if he lives a life of sin, it will soon show in his face and form.

Memory Verse

"Be sure your sin will find you out."—Num. 32:23

HE MISSED THE PARTY

How WOULD you feel about missing a party that was held in your honor? One afternoon a Sunday-school teacher and her class of a dozen small boys decided to give a surprise birthday party for one of the class. The boy's mother was told of the plan and she promised that she would keep the little boy at home so he would be surprised when the guests arrived. Finally the hour came and the teacher and class were all ushered into the home. Then the mother went to the back yard to call her son. "Jacob, Jacob," she called, but there was no answer. The mother went to the barn and called, then to the orchard, then to a neighbor's, but little Jacob could nowhere be found. Of course everyone was disappointed. The mother was very much embarrassed but simply did not know what to do. So the guests had their party without the guest of honor. They played games, ate delicious ice cream and cake, and had a wonderful time. In the late afternoon little Jacob came sneaking into the house. After a great deal of questioning and threatening, the mother found out why he did not answer when he was called. He thought his mother had some work for him, so he hid in the strawstack at the barn and refused to answer.

Now just think what he missed—a wonderful party in his honor. He missed blowing out the candles on the cake, the refreshments, the games, the jolly good time. And in addition, he disappointed his Sunday-school teacher and his friends, and embarrassed his mother. No doubt he was terribly disgusted with himself, and well he might be.

Once upon a time there was a little boy named Samuel, who lived with the priest in the temple. In the night he heard his name called, "Samuel, Samuel." And Samuel replied "Speak; for thy servant heareth." It was God calling Samuel to become a leader of his people. Suppose Samuel had kept silent! The world never would have had his wonderful leadership. God is calling all of you boys and girls to become his helpers in Christian work. Will you answer his loving voice?

Memory Verse

"Speak; for thy servant heareth."—I Sam. 3:10

WHAT THE WATCH TELLS

(PART I)

WHEN JESUS was on earth, he often used very ordinary objects to teach lessons. Some of these objects were flowers, coins, seeds, birds, yeast, a lost sheep, a lamp, and many similar things. No doubt if he lived among us today, he would use modern things to teach great spiritual truths. For instance, a watch.

Sometimes we say that a watch tells time. Really, a watch can't tell anything because it has no voice. And yet there are some things the watch would tell us if it could:

"I have a Maker." The watch didn't just happen. It is the result of many, many years of scientific and mechanical study and work. And somewhere on your watch, perhaps on the face, or on the works, you will find the name of the maker. Perhaps the watch, if it could talk, would go further and tell us of the great Maker of all things, God. The first words of the Bible tell us, "In the beginning God created. . . ." Just as we have to admit that a watch has a maker, so we can't help but see the impress of God in the beauties of the world about us.

"I consist of a case and works." The case is the outward part that we see, the works are hidden from view, but are even more important than the case. People are much like the watch in this respect—we have bodies and we have souls. Too often we judge a person by his body, his outward appearance. But after all, the thing of greatest importance is the soul within.

"I must be useful as well as ornamental." It is not enough to be beautiful without; we must also function as our Maker intended we should. It is not enough to be good; we must be good for something.

"I must be true." This is one of the things we like in a timepiece. We want it to tell the truth. And isn't this one of the things we demand of our friends? Surely, and it is one of the things everybody expects of us.

"I must keep clean." Outside and inside, we want our watches to be clean. A tiny speck of dirt can stop the watch, or make it run im-

17

properly. And a bit of sin in the heart can spoil the beauty and usefulness of our lives.

Memory Verse

"Man looketh on the outward appearance, but the Lord looketh on the heart."—I Sam. 16:7

WHAT THE WATCH TELLS
(PART II)

A LOT OF folks make the mistake of saying that a watch tells the time. The truth is that a watch can't tell anything, as it does not have a voice. It shows the time. However, we have thought about some of the things a watch might tell if it could talk. Now we want to think about some more things the watch might say to boys and girls if it could talk:

"Don't be too fast." Some young people, like some watches, are too fast. This is the term we use to mean they live wild and reckless lives. They like to run around late at night and get into bad company. Such young people often wind up in hospitals and police courts.

"Don't be too slow." Nobody likes a slow watch and nobody likes a slow, mopey, dopey boy or girl who is careless, indifferent, and has no pep.

"We need to be wound regularly." If you fail to wind your watch, it runs down. Everybody knows that. And people need to be "wound up" spiritually or they too will run down. That is why we go to church and Sunday school, and that is why we pray and read God's Word.

"Polishing the case won't help me inside." Everybody knows that, but a lot of people seem to think that fashionable clothes, jewelry, smart hats, and cosmetics make them better than others. They are wrong, of course.

"I want to be regulated by the master clock." It doesn't pay to set your watch by just anybody's. If you set it by everybody's along the way, it will never be correct. The sensible thing is to set it by official U.S. Naval Observatory time. And in regulating our lives, we need to look at the life of our Master, Jesus Christ. He is our great standard. We must bring ourselves into line with him.

Memory Verse

"Man looketh on the outward appearance, but the Lord looketh on the heart."—I Sam. 16:7

DO ANGELS SMILE?

A LITTLE GIRL and her mother were walking in a cemetery, looking at the monuments and tombstones, and reading the inscriptions. It is a very interesting thing to do, and everybody—even boys and girls—needs to think the solemn thoughts one naturally thinks while in the cemetery, which we sometimes call "The Village of the Dead." Well, by and by the mother and little daughter came to a large monument on which there was a statue of an angel.

After looking at the statue for a while, the little girl said, "Mother, I suppose the poor person buried there didn't go to heaven." "Why do you say such a thing?" asked the mother. "Well," said the little girl, "if the person went to heaven, then why is the angel weeping?" Perhaps the little girl was right in the matter. After all, does not the Bible tell us that the angels rejoice when sinners are sorry for their sins? If they rejoice, do they not smile at the same time? And how about the time the angel told the shepherds, "I bring you good tidings of great joy"? Can you imagine even an angel urging people to be very happy while he himself is sad of face? And there are many verses in the Bible which teach us that the angels are always singing praises to God. If they do, surely they must have happiness written on their faces.

On Easter morning the friends of Jesus came to his tomb and found it empty, for Jesus had risen from the dead. Then it was the angel of the Lord told them the good news that Christ had conquered death. Can you imagine that he announced the wonderful news with a sad face? No, indeed. We must always think of the angels as being happy and joyful.

Heaven is not a place where people are sad of heart. The Bible tells us that if we love God and try to do his will we need not have troubled hearts. Jesus has prepared a place for us where we shall always be happy. We read that "God shall wipe away all tears" from our eyes when we get to heaven.

Memory Verse

"In thy presence is fulness of joy; at thy right hand there are pleasures forevermore."—Ps. 16:11

THROUGH THE TUNNEL
(EASTER)

IN THESE days when most families travel in automobiles and busses, a lot of boys and girls are growing up who have never gone through a railroad tunnel. It is a very interesting experience, and it makes one very thoughtful to realize that one is in the very heart of a mountain. Sometimes people are frightened at the idea of plunging into the dark opening in the side of the mountain.

The story is told of a dear old woman who was on her way by train to visit some relatives. The train had to pass through a long tunnel and the very idea of it frightened the poor woman more and more. The conductor just smiled when she expressed her fears, and the other passengers tried to keep her from being afraid, yet she dreaded the thought of passing through the tunnel. By and by she fell asleep, and while she was asleep the train went through the tunnel and she awoke just as the sunshine and beautiful scenery on the other side of the mountain came into view.

Is it necessary to tell you what great spiritual truth this story teaches? Probably you are thinking of how some people are afraid of death. But the Christian need have no fear of plunging into the dark tunnel of death. He knows his heavenly Father will bring him safely through. Death to the Christian is something like falling asleep. When we wake up, we find ourselves in the beautiful place called heaven, which our Savior has been making ready for us.

Memory Verse

"Yea, though I walk through the valley of the shadow of death, I will fear no evil: for thou art with me."—Ps. 23:4

WHO'S AFRAID?

MANY YEARS ago a boy and his father were traveling in the Far West and one night found it necessary to stay in a very crude mountain inn. In the bedroom next to them were two rough-looking men. The father and son became quite alarmed that these men might be robbers and would do them harm during the night. So the father decided to stay up all night in order to be alert if anything happened. He had a gun ready for any emergency. After he put out the lamp, he noticed a streak of light coming through the logs from the room in which the rough-looking characters were staying. So the father peeked through the crack, hoping to see if the men were planning any badness.

After a while the father put his gun away and got into the bed with his son. Then he whispered: "It's all right, Son. Those men may be rough-looking but they are not bad men. When I peeked through the crack, I saw one take a Bible off a shelf and read from it aloud; then they knelt and the other man prayed. People like that are not likely to do us harm."

Now and then people who read the Bible, and pray, and go to church are insincere and even wicked. But generally they are people who can be trusted. A minister once had to wait for a train at a lonely country station. The waiting room was open and lighted, but the agent was not there. After a while a big, powerful man dressed in the roughest kind of clothing and carrying a shotgun came in. For a while the minister was very uneasy. The man put down his gun and started humming an old revival meeting tune. After that the minister was not afraid.

A great surgeon in Baltimore once remarked that he never began an operation without first asking God's help. Perhaps that is why so many people trusted and loved him, and also why he was so successful.

With very few exceptions, people who read God's Word and pray can be trusted.

Memory Verse

"The Lord is the strength of my life; of whom shall I be afraid?"— Ps. 27:1

THE MERRY-GO-ROUND LIFE

THE STORY is told of a little boy who lived in the country. He went to visit his grandmother who lived in a city. Now the grandmother, like most grandmothers, wanted to show her little grandson a good time, so she took him to a carnival that was being held near her home. There were Ferris wheels, shooting galleries, side shows and a merry-go-round. The little boy begged so hard to be allowed a ride on the merry-go-round that his grandmother finally gave him the money and put him on one of the wooden horses.

On their way home the old grandmother said: "Now you've been on that merry-go-round; you've been round and round and round, but where have you been? Nowhere! When it stopped you got off just where you got on."

No doubt the little fellow felt he had been somewhere, his grandmother notwithstanding. All little boys are entitled to at least one ride on a merry-go-round. But unfortunately a lot of young people, and many not so young, live a merry-go-round sort of life. All they want is one round of pleasure after another. The mere fact it gets them nowhere makes no difference—just so it is fun, pleasure, amusement, and thrills.

There is an old saying, "All work and no play makes Jack a dull boy." We might also say that all play and little work makes Jack something worse than a dull boy. He soon becomes a problem to himself, his family, and the community. What young people need to do is learn to properly mix pleasure and work. The life that is all out for pleasure, like the merry-go-round, may be exciting for a while but it gets you nowhere in the end.

Many boys and girls find their greatest pleasure in their churches. The average church has a program that involves social expression and recreation as well as worship. Unless and until young people find Jesus Christ, they begin at no beginning and work to no ending.

Memory Verse

"Delight thyself also in the Lord; and he shall give thee the desires of thine heart."—Ps. 37:4

WORMY APPLES

EVERYBODY LIKES an apple. Some like the Black Twig, some prefer the York Imperial, some like the Grimes Golden, many want the Stayman's Winesap, and so on. But there is one kind of apple that nobody wants—the wormy apple. It makes us shudder even to think of biting into a nice, big juicy apple only to find that a worm or several worms have got there ahead of us.

Have you ever heard how worms get into apples? Some of you boys and girls may have the idea one little boy had. He said the worms just come down the road, see an orchard and sneak in; then they pick out a tree, climb the tree, and start boring into the prettiest and biggest apples they can find. What this little boy didn't know was that worms don't enter the apple from the outside. Those who know tell us that insects carry the egg to the apple blossom in the early spring and plant it there. As the blossom slowly starts to become an apple, the sun hatches the egg into a worm. As the apple grows bigger the worm becomes bigger and more active. It eats at the very heart of the apple, and that stunts its growth, makes it knotty and undesirable. And so the farmers have to spray their trees with something that kills the germs before they get much of a start. If they did not, nobody would buy their apples.

The heart of a boy or girl is very much like the apple. When they are very young, old Satan likes to plant the eggs of sin in their tender hearts. As they grow older these eggs of sin develop into bigger sins. They stunt the spiritual growth of young people, and keep them from being good at heart. And if they keep on with these eggs of sin growing in their hearts, they will be cast aside, just as wormy apples are cast aside.

The thing for boys and girls to do in the "blossom time" of their lives is to ask the Savior to keep them free from the eggs and blight of sin.

Memory Verse

"Create in me a clean heart, O God."—Ps. 51:10

THE MARK OF THE CROSS

SOME PEOPLE are so unfortunate that they have not had even the first few grades in school and therefore cannot read or write. Yet some of these people have to transact business which requires their signatures. Now, how can they sign their names if they can't write? Well, the law has made provision for this. They get someone else to write their names for them and then they make a cross mark beside their names.

The cross mark is in imitation of the cross of Christ, and to make that sign after one's name is the same as saying, "As a Christian I promise on my sacred honor to do this."

What a wonderful thing it would be if everybody who made a promise would keep it! And of all people who should keep their promises, certainly Christians should. A pastor remarked about a young woman who was a member of his church, "She is a very promising young woman." Then he went on to say, with an effort to smile, that she was always quick to make a promise, but seldom kept it. She promised to attend Sunday school and church regularly, but didn't; she promised to help with an entertainment, but failed to do so; she promised to give to the missions budget, but never paid up. Yes, the pastor was right, she was a very promising young woman. Or was she?

Real Christians do what they promise to do, regardless of whether their names are signed to papers, or whether they have made the mark of the cross. When people unite with the church, they stand before God's sacred altar and solemnly promise to take their places and do their duty as Christians in the church. Do they keep their promises? If they did, every pastor's heart would be happy, and church work would go at top speed instead of dragging as it too often does.

It is a very serious matter if we sign a contract of some kind and then do not live up to it. It is even more serious when we promise God to love and serve him, then fail to do it.

Memory Verse

"Thou, O God, hast heard my vows."—Ps. 61:5

A GOOD ACCIDENT

EVERY DAY we hear or read about a bad accident that happened somewhere or other. Have any of you children ever heard of a *good* accident? Well, it is possible that accidents can serve a good and useful purpose.

An outstanding lawyer once held up his hand before an audience and revealed that several fingers were missing. Then he said, "It was a lucky day for me when I lost those fingers in a sawmill accident, for it was then I decided to get an education instead of being just a laborer all my life." A young man's auto skidded on a slippery road and he was sent to the hospital with several broken bones. When he recovered from the accident, he married the nurse who had been so kind to him during his misfortune, and he always felt the accident was one of the best things that ever happened to him.

Then there is the case of a young preacher who was blinded in a hunting accident. Instead of giving up in discouragement, he continued on as a minister and pastor. Many times he told his friends, "That accident was the best thing that ever happened to me. My physical blindness has helped me to *see* some things I could never have seen with my human eyes." Perhaps he meant he could better sympathize with others in distress; or he may have meant his blindness gave him more opportunity to meditate and study about the deep spiritual things of life.

Very often the things we consider to be great misfortunes turn out to be blessings in disguise. There are many stories in Scripture of people who seemed to have bad luck; then after a while God used their misfortunes to accomplish good in their lives and make them a blessing to others. No doubt the great apostle Paul thought it was terrible to be in prison because of his zeal to serve Christ. But while he was in prison, he told his guards of Jesus and many of them were converted. These soldier-guards were sent to faraway lands by the Roman military authorities, and everywhere they went they preached about Christ. Yes, some of our misfortunes turn out to be great blessings.

Memory Verse

"Surely the wrath of man shall praise thee."—Ps. 76:10

A TALKING CHRISTMAS TREE

EVERY YEAR the merchants of a certain city see to it that in the center of the town a very large Christmas tree is erected. It is a thing of beauty, especially at night with its many hundreds of electric lights. One year there were concealed within the tree loud-speakers, or amplifiers, from which music and messages were given to all who would listen. The papers called it "The Talking Christmas Tree." Now it so happens that a good Christmas tree doesn't need amplifiers to help it say something to everybody. Would you like to know some of the things it says to all boys and girls?

"Be upright and straight." Who wants a bent-over, crooked Christmas tree? This teaches us a lesson too. Nobody wants us around if we are crooked, if we are not upright.

"Be evergreen." The pines and cedars are a thing of beauty all the year. They cheer up the countryside. We love them especially because when the leaves are off the other trees, these are green as usual. Evergreen Christians, too, are nice people to have around. Who likes the Christians who are devoted to Christ only in the winter, or during Lent, and who lose all their love for Christ when the summer season comes?

"Be well rounded." Just as we want an upright Christmas tree, so we want one that is well rounded, that is, not lopsided. And by the way, some people are lopsided. They go all out for amusements, or sports, or money-making, or clothes, or this and that. All of these things have their place and their importance, but we must learn to live well-ordered, balanced lives. And no life is well rounded that leaves religion out.

"Make others happy." That's the big job of the Christmas tree. Perhaps no other thing that has ever grown, or been made by the hands of man, has brought more joy to the world. And this is because the Christmas tree reminds us of the joy that came to the world when Christ was born.

Memory Verse
"The righteous . . . shall grow like a cedar in Lebanon."—Ps. 92:12

THANKSGIVING ARITHMETIC

(THANKSGIVING DAY)

A BOY WAS very, very smart in arithmetic. No problem seemed too hard for him. He loved to figure—to add up, subtract, divide, and multiply. His parents and teachers were amazed at his wonderful ability to "juggle" figures.

Well, one day the minister called and he was hardly seated before the boy asked him for an arithmetic problem. Now, the minister was not too bright when it came to arithmetic. At least he had not had much practice counting up money. But he was ready to give the boy a problem to work. He said to the lad, "Count your many blessings." "Just how shall I do that?" asked the boy. Then the pastor told him to put down the number of days in the year, then multiply by the number of hours in a day, then get the number of minutes. That came to 525,600. "Each minute is a blessing," said the pastor, and the boy agreed. "Now," said the pastor, "we take about twelve deep breaths a minute, and each breath is a blessing, so multiply by twelve." The boy was able to give the answer, 6,307,200.

"You're not through," said the minister, as his eyes twinkled. "Now start counting up your friends, and all the flowers, and all the trees, and all the birds, and all the stars, and all the good books, and all the other blessings God in his goodness has given to you."

There was nothing for the lad to do but admit the problem was too much for him, so he gave up, just as any professor of mathematics in a university would have had to do.

Count your many blessings, name them one by one,
And it will surprise you what the Lord hath done.

Memory Verse

"Bless the Lord, O my soul, and forget not all his benefits."—Ps. 103:2

THREE WISE CHILDREN

ALMOST EVERYBODY knows about the three Wise Men who came to worship Jesus when he was a little Babe in Bethlehem. You may wish to learn about three wise children of Bible times. They didn't know each other, and they didn't journey to Bethlehem, but all did something to prove they were truly wise.

The first of these wise children was a little maid whose name we do not know. She was a little slave girl and lived in the household of Naaman, a very important army officer of Syria. Naaman was a great military chief; he seems to have been wealthy, and all the people considered him a very smart man. But Naaman became ill with leprosy, a terrible disease that was considered incurable. Then the little wise girl, Naaman's maid, told of Elisha, a good man of God who lived in Samaria, far away. She also talked about the God of the Jews, who could work miracles, and the result was that Naaman went to Elisha and was healed. Read the Bible story in II Kings 5. It will make you glad to learn how a little slave girl could be so smart, so wise, and so kind.

Another of this trio of wise children was Daniel. He was a Jewish slave boy. Daniel was ordered to drink alcoholic liquor and eat harmful food. Very wisely and very discreetly, he refused to do so. The result was he became handsome in appearance, strong of body, and very intelligent. Boys and girls who do not touch strong drink and eat harmful foods prove by their refusal that they are wise.

The third of these wise children was a little lad who went out with a great crowd of folks to hear Jesus teach. He took with him his lunch. No one else in that great crowd had been so thoughtful. He must have been a sort of Boy Scout, because he believed in the Scout motto, "Be Prepared." That alone showed he was wise, but the test of his wisdom came when Jesus asked the boy for his lunch. Jesus wanted to multiply it by his miraculous power and feed the multitude with it. If the boy had been selfish, he would have refused. But he was a wise boy. He was intelligent. He knew Jesus would do good with it, so he willingly gave it to the Lord.

Those three Wise Men in the Christmas story didn't have anything on these three wise children—Naaman's maid, Daniel, and the lad with the loaves and fishes.

Memory Verse

"The fear of the Lord is the beginning of wisdom."—Ps. 111:10

PIGS IN THE MUD

THE STORY is told of a city man who bought a home in the country. Through his land there ran a small stream of water which the man wanted to use to feed a swimming pool he was having constructed. Unfortunately the water usually was muddy and unfit for swimming. This made the owner very unhappy because he had his heart set on having a nice swimming pool in his meadow. So there seemed to be nothing else to do but call in the experts and find out what would have to be done to make the water pure. The experts analyzed the water, made surveys, and came up with a very expensive plan to eliminate the impurities from the water.

Then one day a neighbor who knew the country very well said to the man, "If you want that water to be pure, all you need to do is to go up the stream a short distance and chase out the pigs that are wallowing there." It was a simple solution to the problem. The pigs were chased out of the stream and kept out, and in a short while the water was clean and pure again. There was no need for the expensive purifying plant.

Sometimes our lives are like that muddy stream. We do and say things that certainly are not becoming to cultured Christian people. Our friends notice it, and we know it ourselves. The thing for us to do is to correct the trouble at its source. We need to get our hearts right with God, and then what we do and say will be pleasing to God, our friends, and ourselves. We don't need to call in the experts, the professors, the psychiatrists; all we need to do is to ask God to help us get "the pigs out of the stream"—in other words, get sin out of our hearts. When our hearts are pure, our words and deeds will be pure.

Memory Verse

"Wherewithall shall a young man cleanse his way? by taking heed thereto according to thy word."—Ps. 119:9

WHAT'S IN YOUR BIBLE?

DID YOU ever hear the story of the minister who was out calling and asked his host for a Bible from which to read before going on his way? Well, the man was very much embarrassed that he couldn't find the family Bible, so he asked his wife to hunt it. Finally she found it, dusted it off (in another room), and brought it to the preacher. When the preacher opened the Bible, a pair of glasses fell out. "Well, I declare," exclaimed the hostess, "there are my glasses I lost four years ago and could never find!" It was evident she hadn't read her Bible for four years. Now what do you think of that?

And then there is the story of the teacher in the kindergarten who asked a child to name some things to be found in the Bible. "Well," she replied, "there are some pressed flowers, a lock of mother's hair when she was a little girl, some clippings from old newspapers, some of mother's recipes, and a page with all of our birthdays." How unfortunate it is that in some homes all the Bible seems useful for is to store things! The story is told of an old man who put money between the pages of his Bible for safekeeping. One night robbers broke into his home and ransacked it from top to bottom. They pulled out all the bureau drawers, poked around in all the cupboards, lifted up the carpets, and looked behind the pictures, but they didn't find his money. It never occurred to them to look in the Bible on the living-room table.

But the Bible is not a place to put things for safekeeping. It is a place from which to get things that will make our lives safe and happy. The Bible is a mine of precious treasure, but we must dig out these treasures. They don't just fall out like the spectacles, or the locks of hair and the clippings. Yes, the Bible is not a place to put things, but to get things.

Memory Verse

"Thy word have I hid in mine heart, that I might not sin against thee."—Ps. 119:11

FOUR MEN AT NIAGARA FALLS

FOUR MEN stood together where they had a good view of that wonder of nature, Niagara Falls. All were looking at the falls, yet each saw something different. One man was an artist, and all he could see was the beauty of the scenery; another man was a farmer, and as he stood there, he thought of how his farm could use some of that water if it could be diverted into irrigation ditches; a third man was an engineer, and as he stood there watching the strong currents, he kept thinking of the wonderful electrical power the falls could generate; the fourth man was a very religious man, and as he stood there he could not help thinking what a wonderful God the great Creator must be, to create such a river and keep it running century after century.

As a rule, we see what we look for. Some people go through life looking only for trouble, and they usually find it. Some people go through life looking only for dirt and filth, and they find it. Have you heard this little verse:

Two men looked through prison bars;
One saw mud, the other stars.

You see, it all depends upon what you are looking for. One of the greatest preachers in American history was Henry Ward Beecher.

At the close of one of his great sermons a schoolteacher went up to him and said, "Dr. Beecher, I counted eighty grammatical errors in your sermon." The critic knew what was wrong with the sermon, but missed what was right with it—its message of love, faith, and salvation from sin.

As we go through life, should we not make it a habit to look for the good, the true, and the beautiful on every hand and in everybody? We shall see it if we look for it.

Memory Verse

"I will lift up mine eyes unto the hills, from whence cometh my help."—Ps. 121:1

BLOSSOMS

ALL OF us are glad it is blossomtime again. It does our hearts good to see the blossoms on the fruit and ornamental trees, to see the springtime flowers and hear the birds sing. Can anything be more beautiful than the apple and cherry blossoms?

If the blossoms could talk out loud, I am sure they would say at least three things to our boys and girls:

Perhaps the first thing they would say is this, "God is love." The florists have a slogan they put into their advertisements, "Say It with Flowers." By this they suggest that flowers help us to tell others of our love for them. That is why we give flowers to the living, and lay flowers on the graves of our dead—to tell of our love. So don't you think that a cherry tree in blossom, or an apple tree, or any of the hundreds of kinds of blossoms are all telling us of the love of God?

Second, the blossoms remind us we must keep growing. The beloved poet Longfellow, when he was past eighty years of age, was asked the secret of his beautiful life and character. He replied by pointing to an apple tree in blossom. "The blossoms on that tree," he said, "are only on the new wood grown in the past year. And so I try to be like that tree, always growing." No matter if our bodies do have to grow old, our spirits may keep young.

"Keep your promises" is the third and last lesson the blossoms have to teach us. Every blossom is a possible apple or peach or cherry, depending, of course, upon the kind of tree it is. A little boy said to his grandfather, "Oh, Grandfather, what a lot of apples those blossoms will bring!" "Yes," said Grandfather, "if they keep their promises." He knew that some might be nipped by the frost, or damaged by rain and sun, and would never mature as fruit. Boys and girls sometimes start out with great promise and then become a disappointment to parents, teachers, and friends. "God is love; keep growing spiritually; and make good your promises." This is what the blossoms are saying to you.

Memory Verse

"The Lord hath done great things for us; whereof we are glad."— Ps. 126:3

LETTING MOTHER DOWN

THIS TALK is about a bad boy who wasn't so bad after all. Eddie was a great problem in the schoolroom. He was always up to mischief. He loved to tease the girls by pulling their pigtails and hair ribbons; he threw spitballs and set pin traps; he neglected his lessons, talked ugly to the teacher, and was in the middle of many a scrap with the other boys. When the principal punished him, he didn't seem to mind it at all.

Then one day Eddie did something worse than anything he had done before—he took something that didn't belong to him. When the teacher accused him, he tried to lie out of it. Stealing and lying go right along together. People who steal tell lies and people who lie will steal.

Well, the teacher was at her wit's end what to do. Finally she said to Eddie, "I'll have to go with you to your home and have a talk with your mother." Then Eddie began to cry, the first time the teacher had ever seen him in tears. After a bit Eddie said, between sobs, "Please, teacher, punish me in some other way but don't tell my mother. You see, mother thinks I am such a good boy and she is so proud of me, and I don't want to let her down." Eddie knew it would almost break his mother's heart to hear how bad he had been, and he would rather take a severe whipping instead.

So the teacher promised Eddie another chance. This time he was determined to be good and worthy of his teacher's kindness and his mother's love. As the days went by he improved as a pupil, was kind to everybody, and put into practice the things he had learned at his church. And all because he didn't want to "let his mother down."

All mothers, and fathers too, want their children to be good. It pains their hearts and destroys their happiness to learn their boys and girls are doing wrong. When we are tempted to do wrong, it will help us a lot to remember how unhappy it would make our parents, who love us so.

Memory Verse

"Forsake not the law of thy mother."—Prov. 1:8

STEERING CLEAR OF THE ROCKS

MANY YEARS ago one of the Presidents of the United States was taking a trip on a Mississippi River steamboat. Being a friendly man, he walked freely among the passengers and members of the crew, and finally found himself standing beside the boat's pilot. How long have you been piloting boats on the river?" asked the President. "Nigh on to forty years," said the pilot. "Then," said the President, "I suppose you know exactly where all the rocks are in this part of the river." "No, sir," was the pilot's reply, "I don't know where the rocks are, but I know where the rocks ain't." The pilot knew where the safe channel was and kept his boats there. He didn't take any chances by getting among the rocks. The commander of the great battleship "Missouri," which was stranded in the mud because it left the deep channel of Chesapeake Bay, could have learned a valuable lesson from this old pilot, don't you think?

And boys and girls might also find his advice worth while. Our lives are very much like boats on the river of life. This river has many dangerous rocks and shoals, some above the surface where we can see them, others just beneath the surface where they cannot be seen. There are some advantages in knowing where the dangers are, but it is of greater value to know where the safe channel is, and keep in it. There may be some value in knowing where the places are that boys and girls get into badness and trouble, but isn't it better to stay in the safe channels marked out by the church and by our loving parents?

That old river pilot may not have had much education in so far as the schools are concerned, but he had learned some things the hard way. We will be wise if we stay in the safe channels and avoid the rocks.

Memory Verse

"In all thy ways acknowledge him, and he shall direct thy paths."—Prov. 3:6

YOU AND YOUR SHADOW

SOME BOYS and girls have learned how to have a lot of fun with shadows. When the sun is at a certain place in the sky and you walk away from it, your shadow makes you look like Humpty-Dumpty. Then when the sun is at another place in the sky, your shadow makes you look like Grand-daddy Longlegs. Some children have tried to catch up with their shadows, but no matter how fast they run, their shadows get there first. Many years ago it was a popular parlor trick to make shadows on the wall with your hands. All people needed for this trick was a white wall and a bright light. By folding their hands in certain ways, and wiggling the fingers, they could make all sorts of animals and fowls with shadows on the wall. Probably these were the first motion pictures.

Sometimes we refer to sorrows and troubles as shadows, because they bring gloom into our lives. If you keep your face toward the sunlight, the shadows will fall behind you.

In the book of Acts we read about the good deeds of the apostles. In one place it is said that the people brought their sick loved ones out into the streets and laid them upon couches, hoping that the Apostle Peter might come along and cast his shadow over them. They believed there were healing qualities in his holy life. In the Crimean War, about 1855, a woman named Florence Nightingale organized nurses to help the wounded soldiers. They loved her so much that it is said they would kiss her shadow on the wall. A great American preacher named Phillips Brooks, who wrote "O little town of Bethlehem" and many other poems, was known far and wide as one who made the shadows flee when he came around. When he died, a Boston newspaper said that when Bishop Brooks came downtown, the streets brightened up. One man gave this as his tribute, "When I met him, I was looking down; when he left me, I was looking up." Are we busy chasing the shadows and the gloom out of others' lives?

Memory Verse

"The path of the just is as the shining light."—Prov. 4:18

FROST ON THE WINDOW

ON A cold winter morning a man was busy scraping frost off his windowpane. It was a very difficult task and he was not doing so well. An hour or two passed and a neighbor happened to drop in. "Why, what in the world are you doing?" asked the neighbor. "I am trying to get this frost off my window so I can see out," was the reply. "You foolish fellow," said the neighbor, "Why don't you build a fire in that stove and warm this room? Then the frost will disappear." And so the story goes, the man built a fire in the stove, the room got warm, and the frost was soon off the window.

It seems silly that anybody would not know the easiest and best way to get frost off a window, but many are just as silly when it comes to making their lives beautiful and attractive. Instead of lighting the fires of Christian love in our hearts, many of us spend our time and money trying to beautify the outside. And so we spend money for jewelry, cosmetics, beauty treatments, and fine clothes, thinking such adornments will make us beautiful. Perhaps they help. Sometimes they have the opposite effect. But if we really want our lives to be beautiful, there is no substitute for building the fires of Christian love in our hearts. Many years ago a wise man said, "Whitewashing the pump won't purify the water." He meant that our words and deeds cannot be good and pure and beautiful unless our hearts are right with God.

The secret of a beautiful, radiant life lies not in "scraping the frost off the window," or in "whitewashing the pump." The secret lies in having the love of Jesus Christ in your heart.

Memory Verse

"Keep thy heart with all diligence; for out of it are the issues of life."—Prov. 4:23

NOT AFRAID OF WORK

IN ONE of our New England states is a swanky boarding school for boys. It is very old, and from the beginning most of its students have been rich men's sons. Many years ago, before the day of furnaces and even stoves, each room of the boy's dormitory was heated by open fireplaces. Each boy was supposed to cut his own wood from the big woodpile back of the building and take care of his own fuel. Some of the rich boys were lazy and preferred to pay to have their wood cut and carried to their rooms.

One day one of these rich boys who didn't know how to work and didn't want to learn went to a teacher and complained, "I can't find anybody to cut my wood for me." The teacher immediately replied, "How much do you pay? I would like to earn a little extra myself." So the teacher rolled up his sleeves and started cutting wood. No doubt he wanted to teach the boy a lesson that work is not disgraceful. And perhaps the boy's face got red with shame.

Those who know about Jesus Christ do not need to be told of the nobility of labor. Jesus was a toiler. The Gospels teach us that he was a carpenter, and a carpenter's son. He knew the meaning of an aching back, of calloused hands and honest sweat. When Jesus selected the men he wanted to be associated with him in building his church and the kingdom of God, he chose men who knew how to earn a living with honest toil. Some of them, you remember, were fishermen. And the Apostle Paul, who did so much to advance the cause of Christ, was a tentmaker, and proud of it.

It might astonish you to learn how many ministers of the gospel have worked their way through college and seminary by very hard toil. Let me mention just one, Peter Marshall, the great Washington pastor, preacher, and once chaplain of the United States Senate. To prepare for his lifework Marshall worked in mines, in factories, and as a laborer with a pick and shovel. Yes, honest toil is something to be proud of, not ashamed of.

Memory Verse

"Go to the ant, thou sluggard; consider her ways, and be wise."
—Prov. 6:6

TEN PLUS SIXTY

How GOOD are you children in arithmetic? For instance, who can tell which is the greater amount, ten plus sixty, or sixty plus ten? "Seventy for both," did you say? Well, you are right, and you are also wrong. This is what I want to impress upon you: if a boy or girl aged ten becomes a Christian and serves Christ sixty years, it is far better than when a person aged sixty becomes a Christian and has only about ten years to serve. You see, the question is just a little tricky, but a great truth is brought to our attention.

Here is another way of presenting this great truth. Let us take seven candles, the smallest one will be about three inches high, the next four, the next five, the next six, and so on to the last one which will be nine inches high. We light the candles and find that all have about the same amount of flame and give the same light. Now we'll let each candle represent a person, beginning with a ten-year-old person and on up to seventy. The question is: "Which candle represents the ten-year-old and which the seventy, and what ages are represented by the others? The first thought of each of us probably is that the smallest candle represents the ten-year-old child, the next represents the twenty-year-old, and so on up to the tallest, representing a person of seventy. But I am sure that if we think a little, we shall see it is just the other way—the shortest candle represents the oldest person because it has only a short while to burn; the tallest candle represents the youngest because it has the longest while to burn.

God is made happy when an old person becomes a Christian, but he is happier when a young person starts to live for him, for the simple reason that ten plus sixty is more than sixty plus ten.

Someone has compiled this interesting chart which we may well call the "Ladder of Life"—"Charming Childhood, Tender Teens, Teachable Twenties, Tireless Thirties, Fiery Forties, Forceful Fifties, Serious Sixties, Sober Seventies, Aching Eighties, Death, the Sod,

God." The main point is that when we are young in years is the best time to give our hearts to God.

Memory Verse

"Those that seek me early shall find me."—Prov. 8-17

MAKING YOUR MARK
(WASHINGTON'S BIRTHDAY)

NEWSPAPERS ONCE told the story of some mischievous boys who went through a public park with some crayons in their hands, and wherever they could find a place to do it, they wrote their names. Within an hour or two they had written their names on many fences, monuments, pavements, and walls of public buildings. When the park policeman finally caught up with them, he made them retrace their steps and erase, or try to erase, all they had written.

Unfortunately it is harder to undo some things than to do them, and it was impossible to clean up all the mess they had made. And while it took them only an hour or two to make the crayon marks, it took them many more hours to try to erase them.

This week we shall celebrate the birthday of a great American, George Washington. His name is carved on more monuments, and more cities and counties are named after him, than any other man who ever lived. He did not go around writing his name in public places; the world has done it for him, and all because he loved his fellows and wanted to help them to the better life.

And so it was with a young man who once lived in a little village called Nazareth. His name was Jesus. He never bothered to write or carve his name. He was too busy going about doing good. And in this way he wrote his name in the hearts of people everywhere—rich and poor, white and colored, educated and uneducated, in every land, in every age.

And so, boys and girls, when you feel the urge to write your name or carve your initials in a public place, don't do it. Remember the better way, which is to write your name in the hearts of people by deeds of love and kindness.

Memory Verse

"The memory of the just is blessed: but the name of the wicked shall rot."—Prov. 10:7

KEEP YOUR TEMPER

ON THE bulletin board of a church was this interesting saying: "Keep your temper; nobody wants it." Here in a few words a great truth is brought home to us. In fact, there are two great truths in the little sentence. The first is that we should keep our tempers. Did you ever think that it is a good thing to have a temper? To be sure, it is. If the spring in your watch did not have temper, it would cease keeping time; if the springs in the pastor's automobile did not have temper in them, the car would ride like a farm wagon; if a razor blade does not have temper, it won't do a very good job taking off Daddy's whiskers. Now a certain amount of temper is good for people to have. I mean by this, life, pep, ambition, and spirit. Such temper we must try to keep.

The second great truth in the little sentence is that nobody likes folks who lose their tempers. We may take this two ways. Nobody likes those who are lacking in ambition and spirit, who are dull and lazy and careless. And nobody likes those who lose their tempers in the sense of becoming angry, and "flying off the handle," and who say mean, ugly, and cutting things.

The noble Abraham Lincoln is supposed to have said, "If angry, count ten before speaking; if very angry, count one hundred." The idea is to give you time to cool off, and not lose your temper.

Someone has suggested that we need yet another organization,

"The League of the Kindly Tongue." The members would be required to refuse to "use words that bite and tones that crush."

Boys and girls, do you have temper? I hope you have. But remember the saying on that church bulletin board, "Keep your temper; nobody wants it."

Memory Verse

"A soft answer turneth away wrath: but grievous words stir up anger."—Prov. 15:1

GIVE YOUR FROWN A REST

MANY PASTORS have seen to it that a snappy sentence appears on the bulletin board of the church. Very few of these sentences are original, but are gathered from many sources. The purpose is to give passers-by something to think about. I could tell you many stories about how people have been helped by these little messages. For instance, one woman was about to commit suicide when she saw a cheer-up message on the church bulletin board that changed her mind.

But our story this morning is about another person. One day a fine automobile stopped in front of the parsonage. The chauffeur opened the door for a stylishly dressed woman to get out. She rang the doorbell and asked the pastor, "Would five dollars buy that motto you have on your bulletin board?" The pastor told her she could have it without cost, and got it for her. She said, "I want to tack it on a bedroom wall for a certain person to see." Perhaps the person she referred to was her husband. Well, I know you would like to hear what the sentence was that she wanted so badly. Here it is: "Smile awhile, and give your frown a rest."

Perhaps some of us need to be reminded to smile. Too many go about with sad, downcast faces and instead of brightening the lives of others, they just add to the world's gloom and sadness. You

43

know, boys and girls, that disease is contagious. Good things are contagious too. A smile is contagious. Here is a little verse by a poet whose name I do not know, but he has shown how a smile can brighten the lives of others:

Smile, friend, smile,
When you smile, another smiles,
And soon there are miles and miles of smiles,
And life's worth while because you smile,
So smile, friend, smile.

Memory Verse

"A merry heart doeth good like a medicine."—Prov. 17:22

ECHOES

ECHOES CAN be very interesting, and they can also be a great nuisance. A church building which cost several hundred thousand dollars was a disappointment to the members because when finished, it echoed what the preacher had to say, and also ruined the music. By spending several thousand dollars more the trouble was partially overcome. But echoes out in the country are great fun, especially for young people. Well do I remember certain places where I went during my boyhood to make echoes. Standing alongside a hill, I would call my name across a little valley, and in a moment the echo would come right back. I also knew a cave called "Echo Cave."

At a place where echoes came back a little girl once became very angry at somebody and screamed, "I hate you." In a moment a voice came back from across the valley, "I hate you." This greatly frightened her. Then her mother said to her, "Tell the echo, 'I love you.'" The little girl did so, and promptly the voice came back, "I love you."

Life is very much like that. It comes back at us in about the same manner we approach it. If we hate, we are hated in return; if we love, we are loved. Once I held a mirror before the face of a little boy. At first he scowled into the mirror, and the image he saw frightened him. But a little later he laughed, and the face in the mirror laughed back.

All of us get many heartaches and disappointments along the way of life, but generally speaking, if we give the world our best, the best will come back to us.

Memory Verse

"A man that hath friends must show himself friendly."—Prov. 18:24

THE FLAG AND THE JUG

A PASTOR once attended a tabernacle meeting conducted by a world-famous evangelist. On that particular night the evangelist preached what he called his "Booze Sermon." It was really a wonderful message, even though the preacher preached in a manner that would not be acceptable in most of our regular pulpits.

After bitterly denouncing King Alcohol and his doings, the speaker did a very spectacular and dramatic thing. With the thousands of people aroused to great enthusiasm, he asked the audience to arise and pay tribute to the Stars and Stripes, our national flag. On the platform was a large American flag, draped gracefully about its pole, down to the floor. Attempting to raise the flag, the speaker "discovered" that a whisky jug was tied to it in such a manner that the flag could not be waved. Needless to say, the audience hissed and booed the liquor people who were guilty of tying the whisky jug to Old Glory.

"What shall I do with the jug?" shouted the evangelist. There was only one answer to that question. "Smash it," yelled the crowd, and bringing an ax from behind the pulpit, he smashed the jug.

Then the flag, rid of its burden and shame, was raised aloft to the delight of all present. Perhaps the evangelist's pulpit manners were not in line with what is generally expected of preachers, but he surely did emphasize his point. And who would deny for a moment that the whisky jug is really tied to our national flag, dragging it down to the dust? Someday the voters will take their ax and will smash the jug to bits. Let us hope that day is not far distant. Too long Old Glory, as we love to call the flag, has been kept from flying "high, wide, and handsome" by the liquor jug.

Memory Verse

"Wine is a mocker, strong drink is raging: and whosoever is deceived thereby is not wise."—Prov. 20:1

WHEN ACCIDENTS HAPPEN

SOONER OR later you will figure in an accident. That is, if you are an average person. Not many people go through life without having some sort of serious accident. Some accidents are not so serious as far as damage is concerned, but they reveal what sort of people we are. For instance, a doctor had parked his car along a curb, and when he tried to get it out, he had great difficulty because other cars were close to both front and rear bumpers. In getting his car out, he smashed the headlight of the car to his rear. The doctor looked for the owner but couldn't find him; then he looked for an officer to report the accident, but none was in sight. So the doctor wrote a note and tied it on a doorknob. It said: "In moving my car I had the misfortune to break your headlight. I am sorry. Please have the damage repaired and send me the bill." To this he signed his name.

In a few days a man came to the doctor's office and said: "I'm the owner of that car you damaged, and I am glad to meet an honest man. I have sickness in my home and need a doctor, and I want an honest and conscientious doctor. I am asking you to take the case. I am able and willing to pay for your services in full."

So, you see, that in one case at least, honesty paid off. But this is by no means an exceptional case. Many thousands have discovered that it always pays to do right.

Accidents will happen to the most careful of us, and sometimes we are responsible, or partly responsible for them. If we are Christians and good citizens we will do two things about accidents. First, we will try to avoid accidents. For instance, good boys and girls will not leave toys on the steps, or sidewalk, or where someone may stumble over them and get hurt. Second, we will be honorable when an accident does happen. If we are to blame, we will acknowledge our responsibility and do all we can to make things right.

Memory Verse

"Even a child is known by his doings, whether his work be pure, and whether it be right."—Prov. 20:11

SHEPHERDS' CROOKS

ALL OF us have seen pictures of shepherds' crooks. Perhaps our favorite picture of Christ is that of the Good Shepherd. In one hand he carries a shepherd's crook, while the other supports a lamb nestling upon his shoulder. And of course we are familiar with the shepherds in the Christmas pageants, who always have their crooks. Other names for the shepherds' crook are "rod" and "staff." The word crook is most generally used because of the crooked, horseshoelike top.

These shepherds' crooks are very useful to the shepherd. With them he protects the sheep from robbers and wild animals; he uses the hook to pull the sheep from water and mud and holes into which they fall; if one sheep gets mean with the others, he hooks it by the leg and pulls it away; he uses the crook to support himself in his long walks, and leans upon it when he is tired; and the hook is used to pull down limbs of fruit trees to within his reach. No doubt any shepherd could tell of many more uses of his crook or staff.

But I want to talk about the crook of the shepherd's crook. How did it get that way? Well, so they tell us, the shepherds go through the forests and select very young and tender trees of ash, maple, oak, and other varieties. They bend them to the shape desired and tie them in a bent position, then let them grow for another year or two. The tree is then permanently bent, so the shepherd cuts it down and whittles it with his knife into a crook or staff.

There is an old saying, "You can't bend an old hickory." By this is meant that when our lives are bent and twisted in youth, they are likely to remain that way always. How important it is that when we are young, we should try to always be straight and upright. Nobody likes or wants crooked characters. The church is here to help boys and girls to grow straight and strong and true.

Memory Verse

"Train up a child in the way he should go: and when he is old, he will not depart from it."—Prov. 22:6

ANTIQUES

SOME TIME ago I was in an antique store just looking around. What an interesting place it was! There were old beds, and tables, and clocks, and dishes, and guns, and pictures, and a wonderful variety of things that belonged to the long ago. Some of the things were very pretty and in good condition, while many articles were just plain junk. It is astonishing how many people will buy junk just because it is old.

There are some antiques that all of us may have that are thousands of years older than anything you can buy at an antique shop.

May I tell you of some of these very old things that are so worth having and preserving?

The Bible is the world's most wonderful antique. After thousands of years it is still intact. Many have tried to tear it apart and get rid of it, but here it is, the most beloved book in the world. There is no other antique to compare with it. An antique collector who doesn't prize the Bible doesn't know much about antiques.

The Ten Commandments are at least 3,500 years old. That ought to make them antiques. Unlike a lot of old things, not one of the Ten Commandments is broken, or even cracked. People break themselves on the Ten Commandments, but the Commandments are as firm as ever.

The Sabbath is an antique. It is as old as creation itself. People who do not appreciate and observe it are putting a light estimate upon one of God's greatest gifts to mankind.

The faith of our fathers is an antique. Our forefathers believed in God, the Bible, in heaven, in hell, in sin, and in redemption through Christ. Some people do not appreciate our ancient faith and would substitute something modern in its place.

The Rock of Ages is also an antique. A great American statesman once said, "I am more interested in the Rock of Ages than in the ages of rock." That was his way of saying that the Creator is greater than what he created.

Memory Verse

"Remove not the ancient landmark, which thy fathers have set."—Prov. 22:28

THE TRAINED SNAKE

IT WOULD be interesting to have some of you children get up and tell us about your pets. I know some of you have kittens or dogs or canaries or maybe a poll parrot. I have even heard of boys who had white rats for pets, and a movie actress who took a little monkey with her everywhere she went. A lot of movie stars make monkeys out of themselves—or donkeys.

But this is a story about a man whose pet was a boa constrictor, one of the largest snakes to be found anywhere, sometimes growing twelve feet long. When the snake was very young, the man found it in the jungle, put it into a bag and brought it to the United States. He made a cage for it and pampered and petted it just as a boy does a dog. Then he hit on the idea of teaching the snake tricks. He would have the snake wind about his body and then unwind. As the snake became older and longer, the man took the snake on the stage to perform for the crowds. The stunt was to let the snake twine itself about his master's body from his heels to his head. Then the trainer would give the command and the serpent would unwind and go back into his den.

This went on for years. Then one day as the man and the snake went through their act before a great crowd of people, something awful happened. When the trainer commanded the snake to unwind, the snake just tightened about him, squeezing him until his breath was gone, then crushing his bones until finally the man fell lifeless before the shocked crowd. The trainer had trusted the serpent too far.

And this is exactly what happens to thousands of people who trifle with alcoholic drinks. For a long while they think they can master drink. They think they can take it or let it alone. Sooner or later strong drink will strangle you, just as the snake strangled the man. It simply can't be trusted. For our memory verse this morning we will take a verse in the Bible that mentions strong drink, and tells what happens.

Memory Verse

"At the last it biteth like a serpent, and stingeth like an adder." —Prov. 23:32

WAITING FOR THE FLOWERS TO FADE

WHAT WOULD you think of a boy who allowed an apple to get half rotten before eating it? What would you think of a little girl who picked a pretty rose and allowed it to wither before putting it in her hair? What would you think of a man who bought a brand-new automobile and kept it in his garage until it was rusty and out of date before driving it? What would you think of a mother who baked a nice cake, then allowed it to get stale and hard before giving it to her children?

Think about these things a few minutes while I tell you a story. A Christian woman was very ill and the doctors were doubtful if she would live. The woman had a young daughter, twelve years old, whom she wanted to become a Christian and a church member. Now it seems the little girl kept putting the matter off. She would tell her mother, "Oh, there's plenty of time. Wait until I am older."

One day the florist brought a lovely bouquet of fresh flowers to the home and the girl was very much interested as the nurse arranged them in a vase. "I know mother will enjoy these beautiful fresh flowers," said the girl. "Perhaps," said the nurse, "but you see I'll not take them into her room for several days." "Oh, you don't mean that, do you?" cried the little girl. "Mother will enjoy the flowers so much more while they are fresh and lovely."

Then the nurse, who was a Christian, taught the little girl a lesson. She told how God wants young people to give their fresh and beautiful lives to him before they fade. I am sure that the sick mother got the fresh flowers, and I am sure the little girl made the hearts of her mother, the nurse, and herself glad by giving herself to Christ and the Church.

Memory Verse

"Remember now thy Creator in the days of thy youth."—Eccl. 12:1

THE LITTLE TEACHER

A MISSIONARY once went into the heart of Africa, visiting the villages and telling the story of Christ and salvation. In one of the villages he entered he discovered that a goodly number of men and women were already Christians and were eager to have him come and give them further instruction. The missionary decided to organize a church, and the day was set for the new members to be baptized and received into the church. Just before the service a little girl came forward and asked the missionary if she too might be baptized and join the church. She was so very young that the missionary hesitated. Then he suggested that she wait until he came again, some months later. At this the village chief, himself one of the converts, stepped forward and said to the missionary: "Please, sir, all we know about Christ was taught us by this little girl. She has been to the mission school where she learned about Christ, and she came back to teach us." Of course the little girl was baptized and received into the church.

From this interesting story we learn, for one thing, the value of the mission school. It is doubtful if any other phase of missionary work results in more converts to Christianity. Thousands of little boys and girls come under the influence of Christian teachers and go back to their homes and villages to live for Christ and to testify for Christ.

Another great truth is presented to us here. A little child can be used by God to bring many older persons into the Christian fellowship. This is true of not only the mission field, but right here where we live. Almost any pastor can tell you of mothers and fathers, and even families, who have been won to Christ through the influence of little children.

Boys and girls, you don't have to wait until you become men and women before being soul-winners. If a little black girl in the African jungle can win most of her village to Christ, surely you can do the same with those in your home, or neighborhood, who now pay no heed to the claims of Christ.

Memory Verse
"A little child shall lead them."—Isa. 11:6

A LAMB IN THE COLD

I AM NOT so sure whether this sermonette is for children or parents. Maybe it is for both. Well, the story goes that a little boy wanted to be a Christian and join the church. But his parents said no. They said he was too young, and should wait several years until he had reached the age they thought he should be before becoming a Christian and a church member. Now it happened that the boy's parents were farming people. One evening the farmer told the boy to go down to the sheeppen and see that all the sheep were safely inside for the night. It was wintertime, and the little boy did as he was told. When he came in from the snow and cold, his father asked if he had got all the sheep into the fold for the night. "All except a lamb," the boy replied. "Why did you not put that one into the fold?" asked the father. "Well, Daddy, I guess for the same reason you won't allow me to join the church, it was too young." Of course the father went immediately and put the lamb inside the fold. Then he went back to the house and had a long talk with his wife. The next day the father said to the little boy, "Well, son, I suppose it makes as much sense for you to be taken into the church as it does to put the lambs into the fold, so you may do as you desire." That made the lad very happy and soon he was a full member of the church.

One wonders where this idea got started—that children should wait until they are almost men and women before becoming Christians. Jesus pleaded with parents to bring the little children to him, and he warned them of awful punishment if they put a stumbling block in their way.

The old notion that lambs should be kept out in the cold until they become sheep has passed out. The churches everywhere are taking better care of the lambs of the flock.

Memory Verse

"He shall gather the lambs with his arm, and carry them in his bosom."—Isa. 40:11

A MEAN TRICK

THERE IS an old fable that the birds once had a "field meet." They decided to see which one could fly highest into the sky. And so they lined up, birds of every description—big, little, medium, black, red, blue, yellow, and white. The big eagle laughed at all the rest. He was very self-confident. Soaring high was the one thing he knew he could do well. He knew his great strength, and that he was perfectly at home in the high altitudes.

And so off they flew. Up and up they went, climbing higher and higher. One by one their strength gave out and they had to give up and come back to earth, but not that great eagle. He kept going up until he could hardly be seen, and all the other birds were far below. Then in bird language he said out loud, "Well, I won that contest easy enough." "Oh, no you didn't," said a little wren, "for I am higher up than you." What happened was that the little wren was riding "piggyback" on the eagle, and the eagle didn't know the wren was there. I suppose the little wren won the prize.

Now what do we learn from this story of the eagle and the wren?

First, it is all right to try to get up in the world. This is a noble ambition for human beings to have as well as birds. Too many are satisfied to creep along on low levels. They never try to rise above their environment.

The second thing is that we ought to use our brains as well as our muscles. That is what the little wren did. It couldn't compare with the eagle when it came to muscle and strength of body, but what it lacked in strength it made up in intelligence. Many a schoolboy not yet in his teens has an I.Q. greater than the most powerful prize fighters.

But, after all, the little wren's trick was both mean and dishonest, and our third lesson from the incident is, never take an unfair advantage of another. It is poor sportsmanship to rise in the world by trickery. Better it is to play the game according to the rules.

Memory Verse

"They that wait upon the Lord shall renew their strength; they shall mount up with wings as eagles."—Isa. 40:31

WHAT A PARTY!

EVERYBODY LIKES a party. We like the games, the decorations, the refreshments, and everything else that goes along with it. But can you imagine having a good time at a party if you would be the only one there? A lot of the fun comes from seeing others have fun.

There was a little girl who had the queerest tea party. Somebody has written a little poem about it and I shall read it to you. I am sorry I do not know the author's name.

I had a little tea party
This afternoon at three.
'Twas very small—three guests in all—
Just I, myself, and me.
Myself ate all the sandwiches,
While I drank up the tea.
'Twas also I who ate the pie
And passed the cake to me.

I just can't imagine any little girl enjoying a tea party unless there were other little girls and boys there to enjoy it. Yet there are many people, old and young, who are very selfish. They would be very happy to eat all the sandwiches, drink all the tea, eat all the pie and the cake. Indeed, I remember a lad in a Boy Scout camp whose mother brought him a large layer cake. She meant for him to treat the other boys, but he took the cake out into the woods and tried to eat it all without giving the others a taste. He became quite ill and nobody was sorry. Nobody likes selfish people. I doubt if they like themselves.

The true Christian does not go through life ever seeking something for his own enjoyment. Rather, he gets happiness by making others happy.

Memory Verse

"Seekest thou great things for thyself? Seek them not."—Jer. 45:5

HOW RIVERS GET CROOKED

SOME OF you children are studying geography, or at least you have looked at road maps got out by oil companies for motorists. No doubt you have noticed that just about every river on the face of the earth is crooked. One may go along in a straight course for a few miles, but soon it is winding and twisting again. It is said the river Jordan is over two hundred miles long, but if it went on a straight line from where it begins to where it ends, it would be only about eighty miles.

"Have you ever wondered how rivers get crooked? They get that way by "following the line of least resistance." They always hunt the easy way, and always are on the downgrade. When a stream comes to a mountain, or even a hill, it goes around it.

Boys and girls, men and women get crooked the same way rivers do—by "following the line of least resistance." In other words, by always hunting easy jobs, or easy ways to get along. This desire to get by without work and effort causes many sins. It makes you neglect the church, the Bible, and prayer. It encourages dishonesty, stealing, and the telling of lies. It is a sad day in anybody's life when he decides to try to get by in the world without effort. One time a hobo was asked how he decided which way to go. "That's easy," he said, "in the morning when I get out of the hay or straw where I slept during the night, I go out of doors and find out which way the wind is blowing, then I always go with the wind on my back." And that is why he was a hobo. It is not ease, but effort, that brings out the finer qualities within us. Kites always rise against the wind, not with it. "Looking for a soft job is a job for a soft man." "There are no elevators in the House of Success; you must toil up the steps, one at a time."

Memory Verse

"Woe to them that are at ease in Zion."—Amos 6:1

LITTLE THINGS

TODAY, AS never before in history, people know the importance of little things. A few years ago an airplane dropped the first atom bomb. This bomb was many, many times more powerful than any other bomb that had ever been built, and it destroyed thousands of lives and many millions of dollars' worth of property. Yet its great power came from the atom, which is so small that no one has ever seen one. Many years ago someone carelessly tossed a burning cigarette under a store counter. The result was the great Baltimore fire of 1904 that destroyed much of the downtown area of the city. Doctors know the importance of little things. That is why they caution about germs, and scratches, and the cold that hangs on. Merchants know the value of little things, and some great fortunes have been built by the sales of five- and ten-cent articles. Every automobilist knows how a tiny nail can let the air of his tire, or how a speck of dirt can clog the carburetor. And all of us know how a tiny cinder in the eye can take all the joy out of life.

Jesus knew the importance and value of little things. He saw a poor widow put a few pennies in the collection and commended her for what he considered to be a wonderful gift. He took the lunch of a little boy and multiplied it until it could feed thousands. When his disciples refused to let little children come to Jesus, he scolded them for it and said, "Suffer little children to come unto me, and forbid them not." Jesus knew they would grow into manhood and womanhood. He saw their possibilities. Jesus told his followers to sow the seeds of the gospel with the promise that by and by they would reap a rich harvest.

David Everett wrote:

> Large streams from little fountains flow,
> Tall oaks from little acorns grow.

Sometimes we think there is not much that boys and girls can do for the Lord. That is a mistake. From earliest Bible times come true stories of such children as Isaac, Samuel, Naaman's maid, David, the boy Jesus, and others whom God used to his glory. And God can use us in many ways to help his cause along.

Memory Verse

"Who hath despised the day of small things?"—Zech. 4:10

A "GOOD SAMARITAN" DOG

ALL OF us love the story Jesus told about the good Samaritan, the man who helped the poor, wretched fellow who had been beaten by robbers and left in the ditch to die. The ceremonious priest and aristocratic Levite passed by on the other side of the road, while the

Samaritan, a man with not much of a religious background, and what we might call a mongrel ancestry, was the one who cared enough to give the bleeding, dying man some help.

But this is a story about what we might call a "good Samaritan" dog. The story appeared in the newspapers. It seems that a mongrel dog was not eating the food his owners set out for him. He would take the bones, and anything else he could hold in his mouth, and disappear into the bushes. At first the dog's master thought he was burying the food to be eaten later, or was eating it where he couldn't be seen. But the thing kept up, and so one day the dog's owner followed to see what was going on. And what do you think? The dog had been carrying food to another dog that had been trapped in some barbed wire. He was taking his own food to a comrade in distress. He was denying himself what he needed so that another dog could have at least the comfort of enough to eat.

Someone made the remark that the dog's act was "almost human." I am afraid that too few human beings do such things. Some, but not many, go without food so that others in distress may have to eat.

Why did this mongrel dog do such a thing? Did he do it for applause, or compensation, or because he felt compelled to do it? No, he did it because of an instinct God had put within him.

And note that he was just a mongrel dog, not a well-bred, highly pedigreed dog that won blue ribbons at dog shows. And some of the most kind, most gentle, most sympathetic people in the world can't boast of what the world calls blue-blooded ancestry. God bless all the people who share their blessings with others, who feel so sorry for the unfortunate that they are willing to do without things themselves so others less fortunate may have a chance at happiness.

Memory Verse

"Blessed are the merciful: for they shall obtain mercy."—Matt. 5:7

THE DIRTY WINDOWPANE

IT IS hard to believe, but once upon a time a little girl told her mother she wanted to help with the house cleaning. The astonished mother said, "All right, dear, that is wonderful of you. Maybe you would like to go out on the front porch and wash the windows. So the little girl got a bucket, soap, water, and rags and went outside to wash the windows. After a long while the mother went outside to see how her little helper was getting along, and what do you think? The little girl who had started out so cheerfully was almost in tears. "Why, what is the matter?" asked the mother. The little girl replied, "Well, Mommie, I have been washing and rubbing on one windowpane for a long, long time and there is one dirty spot that just won't get clean." The mother looked to see what was wrong, and what do you think the trouble was? You guessed it; the dirty spot she was trying to make clean was on the inside of the glass. No amount of rubbing on the outside could ever have cleaned it inside. So the little girl went inside, washed the soiled spot, and then she was very happy over the beautiful work she had done.

Do you think the little girl should have known better? Perhaps. But isn't it true that a lot of people, old and young, are doing pretty much the same thing with their characters? It is surprising how many people are working hard to make their lives and characters appear clean and beautiful, yet doing it the wrong way. Many are trying to accomplish it with education, culture, fashionable clothing, and the kind of helps sold at cosmetic counters. These things may all have their place, but the real place to begin is within the heart. No amount of polishing the outside of one's life will make us clean and beautiful unless we first make the inside clean and beautiful.

Jesus does not like people who spend time and money improving the outside of their characters while not bothering to make their hearts clean and beautiful. He calls such folks hypocrites. Read Matt. 23:23-29, and if you do not understand the big words you read there, ask Mother and Father to help you.

"Blessed are the pure in heart: for they shall see God."—Matt. 5:8

A LIGHT AT THE WINDOW

AN ARTIST was once employed to paint a picture to be called "Christmas Cheer." If you were asked to paint such a picture, what would it show? I have an idea it would show old St. Nicholas making a lot of little children happy with toys and goodies, or maybe a jolly sleighing party over the hills to Grandfather's house, or it might be some carol singers around a Christmas tree. But this artist painted a picture of a house deep in a forest. The shadows of the night made everything gloomy and forbidding and cheerless.

As the artist neared the completion of his picture, his employer came in and took a look at it. "Why, man," he almost shouted, "there's no cheer in that picture. It's a good picture of gloom," he said. "Just wait," said the smiling artist, "I am not quite through." Then he took up his brush and put a dab of bright yellow paint in each window of the house, and followed with some streaks of light out into the forest. The whole picture was transformed by the light within the house, shining out of the windows. The forbidding-looking house became attractive and inviting. Passers-by could not but get the impression that the house was filled with Christmas cheer; the people were happy, little children were shouting with joy over their toys, and a traveler would find a welcome if he knocked at the door.

Should it not be so with our lives? The world about us may be dark and forbidding, and our own human bodies may be none too attractive. Yet when Jesus shines in our hearts, our lives are made bright. We scatter good cheer. We brighten the pathways of others. We make others think kindly thoughts.

Many years ago a wayward boy ran away from home and never wrote to his loving Christian parents. The mother said, "I will light a lamp each evening and put it in the window so he will know he is welcome home." For fifteen years she did just that. One night there came a knock at the door and the prodigal son had returned. He saw the light in the window and knew it was meant for him. He repented of his wrongs and became a noble Christian worker.

Memory Verse

"Ye are the light of the world."—Matt. 5:14

A GOOD SCOTCH STORY

I KNOW A lad who makes a hobby of collecting Scotch stories, and here is one for his collection. A man was walking down a street of a city in Scotland and saw a boy with a small mirror catching beams of sunlight and reflecting them into an upstairs window of a house on the shady side of the street. This aroused the man's curiosity, and after a while he went to the boy and asked him what he was doing.

"Sir," replied the boy, "my brother is in that upstairs room, sick in bed. No sunlight ever shines into the room because it is always shaded, so every day I come out here and send some rays of sunlight into the room with this mirror."

Isn't that a good Scotch story? If nothing else, it shows how a Scottish lad was thrifty with God's sunlight and wanted to keep it from going to waste. After all, should we not be doing something just like that? There is so much darkness, gloom, ignorance, and superstition in the world, and it is our duty to reflect the light of the gospel of Christ wherever we go. Millions of people are living in darkness in heathen lands, and all about us, and we should get great pleasure out of brightening up their hearts and their homes.

Our pocket mirrors may not always be able to catch and reflect this sunshine, but there are other ways of doing it. By reading the Word of God, attending services in God's house on God's day, singing the songs of the church, and by prayer and fellowship with God's people our hearts are brightened. Should we not then try to reflect that light into the hearts of those less fortunate than ourselves? We can do it by kind words, kind deeds, and generous giving of gifts. Just a few dollars sent to the mission field may be the means of filling some little child's life with the sunshine of God's love.

Memory Verse

"Let your light so shine before men, that they may see your good works, and glorify your Father which is in heaven."—Matt. 5:16

BOY WANTED!

A BANK NEEDED a boy to run errands and to make himself generally useful. The job itself was not important, but there were opportunities for advancement. Many a bank official has started as a messenger or office boy. Some great railroad presidents started out by carrying water for track hands.

Well, the bank advertised for a boy and quite a few answered the advertisement. To each boy who applied the president said, "Can you come to my home Sunday morning at eleven o'clock for an interview?" One by one the boys said they would be there. However, one boy said, "Sir, I am sorry I can't come to your home on Sunday morning. You see, sir, the hour you name is the hour for services at our church and I would not like to miss the service. Then, sir, my parents have taught me not to talk business on Sunday."

Very much to the boy's surprise the president answered, "Well, you are the boy I want. I asked that you come to my home on Sunday at eleven o'clock only to see if you were a church boy, and if you respected the Sabbath day. It has been my experience that we can trust boys who have respect for God and for God's day. You have the job."

Another story concerns William McKinley. When he was President of the United States, he sent a telegram to a retired general stating that he was planning to call on him on a certain Wednesday evening. President McKinley was surprised to get this telegram in reply: "Come before eight o'clock or after nine o'clock, because I always go to prayer meeting at my church on Wednesday evening." Instead of being displeased, President McKinley honored the old general who had such strong religious convictions and principles.

The really important and great people of the world honor those who have religious convictions and stand by them.

Memory Verse

"Seek ye first the kingdom of God, and his righteousness; and all these things shall be added unto you."—Matt. 6:33

FREE AIR

ALL ALONG our streets and highways are gasoline stations, and at almost every one of them you will see a sign, "Free Air." Air always has been and always will be free in this wonderful world of ours. Then why should the filling stations tell us we may have free air? The answer is that it costs money to buy the machines and furnish the service that puts air into our tires. What the advertisements really mean is that motorists may have the free use of these machines and men to keep their tires inflated. Of course the charge for the gasoline and oil makes it worth their while to give us the free air.

One time a man went to his pastor and said, "Pastor, I object to so many offerings in our church. The Bible teaches us that salvation is free, but it costs us plenty here." The patient pastor said, "Brother, the water you drink and with which you bathe is free, but it costs money to build reservoirs, and pipe it into your kitchen and bathroom. It costs money to maintain the water system. And so it is with the love of God, it is free for the world. Yet it costs money to build and maintain churches, and Christian colleges, and to send missionaries to the faraway places of the earth to tell the story of the gospel."

It is true that salvation is free. It is the gift of God. It cannot be bought with money. On the other hand, if we have experienced the wonderful grace of God in our hearts, we will want to share it with others, and this sharing costs money. We can't send Bibles to the non-Christian world without cost; we can't send doctors and nurses to them, and equip hospitals for them, and schools to teach them, without giving money to the church for those purposes.

Yes, salvation is the gift of God—it is as free as the air you breathe. Yet to carry out the command of Jesus, "Go ye into all the world, and preach the gospel," costs money. Those who really know the value of God's wonderful gift to us are the last to complain about the cost of sharing it. It makes our hearts glad to be privileged to do so.

Memory Verse

"Freely ye have received, freely give."—Matt. 10:8

FEATHERS

ONCE UPON a time, so the story goes, a woman confessed to the parish priest that she was guilty of gossiping. She had told a lot of unkind and untrue tales about her neighbors in the village.

The priest told her she must do penance for the sins she had committed, for it really is a sin to tell untruths, and even to speak unkindly. To do penance means to be punished. The priest said: "Take a bag of feathers and go all over the town and put a few feathers in everybody's yard, then come back to me." "That's easy," thought the woman, so she took the bag of feathers and went all over the village, putting a few in everybody's yard, then she went back to the priest and said she had completed doing her penance. "Ah, no," said the priest, "I want you now to go back over the same route and gather up all those feathers." "But I can't do it," said the woman, "by this time the wind has blown them in all directions."

Then the priest explained how impossible it is to recall lies and gossip after they are spoken. There is a little verse Will Carleton has written that tells this same great truth. Here it is:

> Boys flying kites haul in their white-winged birds,
> You can't do that way when you're flying words.
>
> . . . .
>
> Thoughts unexpressed may sometimes fall back dead;
> But God himself can't kill them when they're said.

Memory Verse

"Every idle word that men shall speak, they shall give account thereof in the day of judgment."—Matt. 12:36

THE BETTER WAY

HAVE YOU heard the old fable about the sun and the wind getting into an argument? Well, it seems that each claimed to have the most power. After arguing the matter for a while, they decided to make a test and see which really did have the greater strength. A man was walking along a country road, so the sun said to the wind, "Let me see you blow that man's coat off." Then the wind got busy. It blew, and roared, and moaned, and whistled, and became cold, but the man's coat stayed where it was. Indeed, he buttoned it up, turned up the collar, and wrapped it around himself so tightly that finally the wind just had to give up. The wind simply could not blow the man's coat off. Then the sun went to work. Brightly it shone, gradually becoming warmer and warmer. At first the man turned down his collar, then he unbuttoned the coat, and before long he took it off and carried it on his arm. The sun had won the contest.

The sun won the contest because it had the right idea. It said, "I will make the man *want* to take his coat off." The wind tried to do it by force, the sun by persuasion. This reminds us of the old saying, "You can catch more flies with honey than with vinegar."

Here is a lesson children ought to learn early in life, that persuasion is always better than force. We can't get things done by anger, and scolding, and by being noisy, and bossy, and mean. Such tactics merely make people resentful. It is so much better to warm their hearts with love and kindness, and in that way make them want to do the thing that is to be done.

Sometimes pastors and church workers try to get people into the church by telling them of the awful punishment they will receive if they stay away from God. But Jesus had a better idea. His plan was to warm the hearts of the people by telling them of the wonderful love and kindness of God, and in that manner make them want to be Christians.

Memory Verse

"Then shall the righteous shine forth as the sun."—Matt. 13:43

A KING IN NEED

As JESUS was about to enter Jerusalem on the first Palm Sunday and be proclaimed a king, he sent several of his disciples to borrow a donkey and a colt for his use in the processional. "If any man say aught unto you, ye shall say, The Lord hath need of them," he said. And that is how the Master secured the beasts for his triumphal entry.

A young girl of a large family was a cripple. Her brothers and sisters seemed to care little for her and this made her very unhappy. She felt so useless, and in the way. Then one day she read the

Palm Sunday story and was impressed by the fact that the King felt the need of a donkey. "Well," said she, "if Jesus could make good use of a donkey, maybe he could use me." It put new courage into her heart. Soon she found herself engaged in distributing Bibles and Christian literature, with her home as headquarters and her friends as assistants. When she died forty years later, she was beloved by thousands and had been instrumental in leading many to Christ.

Sometimes we feel we have so little of value to offer the King, yet the King makes it plain that he cannot carry on his work without us. Back in Old Testament times God used the voice of a little slave girl to send the great Syrian captain to the man of God to be healed of leprosy, and God used a little boy, his slingshot and a stone from the brook to kill a wicked giant. Jesus told his disciples he needed food for the hungry masses. All they could find was the lunch of a little boy—five loaves and two fishes. Jesus used this food to feed thousands. A poor widow cast a few pennies into the Lord's treasury, thinking they had little value to the good work. Yet the Master paid her a wonderful compliment for her gift. It is true that God has no hands but ours to do his work, no feet but ours to run his errands, no voices but ours to speak his messages of love to the world. Boys and girls can help—"The Lord hath need of them."

Memory Verse

"The Lord hath need of them."—Matt. 21:3

YOUR MONEY OR YOUR LIFE

MANY YEARS ago, when the United States was still very young, word reached the eastern states that people living in California were finding gold, and lots of it. That caused thousands of people to dispose of their homes, load their possessions in wagons, and go west. There were many dangers to be faced. The roads were very poor; there were awful mountains to be crossed, and wide, sandy deserts; there were wild animals and Indians to contend with; and many of the people died on the way because of illness without medical help. When they got there, only a few really found gold.

Well, the story goes that one man found a lot of gold and decided to come back east to spend it. As he and others were crossing the Mississippi River, the boat struck a rock and sank. It was near enough to the shore for many who could swim to save themselves, yet many drowned, among them the man who had struck it rich. Now he was supposed to have been a good swimmer and the survivors wondered that he should drown. Then they discovered that about his waist he had a belt of many pockets, all crammed with gold nuggets. The weight was too much for him and caused him to drown. There was time to do it, but he didn't want to give up that gold, so he allowed it to carry him down to a watery grave.

Thousands are just like this poor man. They become so attached to their wealth, or so much interested in the things of this world that they lose their precious souls. Many are working so hard to become rich that they lose their health, and their interest in God, the Bible, and the church.

It was a terrible tragedy when the miner lost his life because he was unwilling to give up his gold. It is no less a tragedy when anybody becomes so interested in the things of the world that he no longer has time to look after his spiritual safety.

Memory Verse

"What shall it profit a man, if he shall gain the whole world, and lose his own soul?"—Mark 8:36

JESUS AND THE CHILDREN

A GREAT ARTIST had just completed a painting which he called "Jesus and the Children." The picture portrayed the loving Savior sitting, and all about him were grouped little children, some were standing, some sitting on the ground, and one was on his knee. The Master's face was smiling, and the little children knew that he was their friend.

But there was one thing wrong with the picture—all the children were little white boys and girls. Some Christian people called the artist's attention to this fault in the picture, and he at once set about correcting it. Patiently and carefully he transformed the children grouped around Jesus into children from all races—white, black, yellow, red, and brown. With this correction the picture became very famous and much loved by sincere Christian people everywhere.

Yes, Jesus loves all the little children, of all races and of all lands. When Jesus was on earth, he was never too busy with older folks to take time to talk with little boys and girls. No doubt he would pat them on the head and say a kind word to them as he prayed his Father's blessings upon them.

One thing the boys and girls of the white race ought to remember is that God loves the whole world, all the people everywhere, and has sent Jesus to be their Savior. The blackest little black boy in the heart of Africa is as dear to the Lord as the whitest little white boy anywhere in the world.

Having heard about the artist and his picture, C. H. Woolston, a Baptist preacher, wrote a hymn to be sung to the tune of "Tramp, Tramp, Tramp, the Boys Are Marching." Here is one stanza of the hymn:

Jesus loves the little children,
All the children of the world;
　　Red and yellow, black and white,
　　They are precious in His sight,
Jesus loves the little children of the world.

Memory Verse

"Suffer the little children to come unto me, and forbid them not; for of such is the kingdom of God."—Mark 10:14

UNCONDITIONAL SURRENDER

WHEN THERE is a war, we hear a great deal about armies and soldiers having to surrender. That means they give themselves up to the will of the victorious foe.

But I am going to talk about another kind of surrender, and to get started, let me tell a story. In 1837 a boy was born in Massachusetts. His parents named him Dwight. The family was very poor and little Dwight grew up without much of an education, although he wanted it badly. While he was still a boy he got a job in a shoe store, helping keep it clean and carrying bundles. One day his Sunday-school teacher came in and had a long talk with him. The teacher said, "I want you to surrender your life to Jesus Christ." And right there in the shoe store the teacher and Dwight knelt down and he gave his heart to Christ.

Later on he heard a preacher say, "The world has yet to see what can be accomplished by one man who is completely surrendered to Jesus Christ." Down in his heart Dwight said, "I will be that man." And so it was that Dwight L. Moody became a world-famous evangelist who brought thousands to Christ and inspired the building of hundreds of churches, to say nothing of the schools of religion he was instrumental in starting. Although he has been dead many years, people still love to read his books of sermons and addresses.

What was the secret of his wonderful, useful life? Just this. He was completely surrendered to Jesus Christ. It is said that on the flyleaf of his Bible he wrote these words: "I can't do everything, but I can do something; what I can do, I ought to do; and what I ought to do, with God's help I will do."

Here is another motto I think every Christian should have: "Thy will—nothing more; nothing less; nothing else."

Memory Verse

"They forsook all, and followed him."—Luke 5:11

71

PRAYERS IN A WAGON

WHOEVER HEARD of prayers being loaded in a wagon? Well, this is a story about a wagonload of prayers. It seems that a poor man who lived in the country had an accident and broke his leg. That meant he was laid up for a long while, unable to work. His family was large and he had saved no money. Someone thought it would be a good idea to hold a prayer meeting at the church to pray for the family. The announcement was made, and the night came to hold the prayer meeting. One after another the people asked God to help the family, to send them food and otherwise care for their needs.

Suddenly there was a loud knock on the door and someone tip-toed to the door, opened it, and there stood a young farm boy who said, "My dad could not attend this prayer meeting tonight, so he just sent his prayers in a wagon." And there was the wagon, loaded with pumpkins and potatoes, meat, canned goods, apples, and many other products of the farm. No doubt the people in the prayer meeting felt very much ashamed of themselves for asking God to do for the poor man what they themselves should have done. The farmer who sent his "prayers" in a wagon may not have been exactly correct in his way of doing things, but somehow we all feel the good Lord was satisfied with his noble act. The truth is, children, that often we waste time asking God to do things which we ought to be doing ourselves. Someone has said that if it is not worth while to try to answer our own prayers, we should not bother God with them. Perhaps that farmer should have attended the prayer meeting at his church, but if he was absent because he was busy loading his wagon for the poor man, we can feel sure the Lord excused his absence.

Memory Verse

"Why call ye me, Lord, Lord, and do not the things which I say?"—Luke 6:46

WHY FRANK WAS PUNISHED

WHEN I was a schoolboy the public-school teachers made more use of paddles and switches than they do now. Most of us had a very high respect for those paddles, which we sometimes called "persuaders." Well, one time the whole class, excepting one big, fat, lazy boy who was fast asleep, noticed the teacher pick up her paddle and quietly tiptoe down a side aisle, then come up from the rear. Suddenly she grabbed lazy Frank by the coat collar and proceeded to give him a paddling I know he has never forgotten. In the midst of the excitement Frank cried out, "I didn't do anything, teacher, I didn't do anything!" "And that," said the teacher, "is exactly what I am whipping you for." She had assigned some desk work to the class but Frank decided to take a nap instead. He had done the same thing before, and finally the teacher's patience was exhausted.

I wonder how many of us ever think that it is possible to sin against God by leaving things undone? When children fail to do what their parents and teachers order them to do, it is an act of disobedience and the children need to be punished. And the same thing is true with respect to our heavenly Father's commandments. Jesus taught us that many people will be punished in eternity not for what they did that was bad, but for what they failed to do that was right. Jesus didn't accuse the priest and Levite in the good Samaritan story of doing anything wrong; they just failed to help the poor man who had been beaten and robbed. In the parable of the talents Jesus didn't condemn the one man for any definite, sinful act. He condemned the man for not using his talent as he had been instructed to do. Then do you remember how Jesus condemned a fig tree for bearing no fruit, and caused it to wither away?

Indeed, we must be doing God's will day by day. Being a Christian doesn't merely mean being good. We must do good as well as be good. Someone has said:

> Count that day lost whose low descending sun
> Views from thy hand no worthy action done.

"These ought ye to have done, and not to leave the other undone."—Luke 11:42

SEARCHING FOR HAPPINESS

JUST ABOUT everybody in the world is seeking happiness. But not all are seeking it where it may be found. Some think that in order to be happy they must have a lot of money, or a great palace, or a big automobile, or expensive clothing, or wonderful jewels. Some seek happiness in strong drink, in rare foods, and sinful living.

I once knew a boy who loved pretzels very much. He spent all his pennies for pretzels. One day he said that his idea of complete happiness would be to work in a pretzel factory with no limits being placed on the number of pretzels he could eat.

There is an old, old story about a king who was very unhappy. He had everything his heart could desire, yet he was downhearted. He had a wonderful palace, a lovely queen, thousands of servants, untold treasures, gilded chariots, private entertainers, but they couldn't make him happy. One day a wise old man said to the king, "If you can find a perfectly happy and contented man, then borrow and wear his shirt for three days, and you will be happy." So the king sent messengers in all directions to try to locate a perfectly happy and contented man, but they came back without success. Then the king himself started out in search of a happy man. One day he saw a poor peasant working in a field. He was whistling and singing as he went about his work. "Are you perfectly happy?" asked the king. "Yes," said the poor laborer, "why shouldn't I be? I have a good wife, six fine, healthy children, a comfortable cottage and enough to eat. I am perfectly happy."

Then the king asked the man for the loan of his shirt, only to discover the man didn't have a shirt. So the king learned a great lesson that day. He learned that true happiness does not come with riches, and all the conveniences of wealth. True happiness comes from within. The happiness this world gives is not enduring. The only happiness that we can carry along into eternity with us is that which comes from knowing and doing the will of God. Some of the happiest people in the world are very poor. Andrew Carnegie once said he knew a lot of millionaires, but only a few of them ever laughed.

Memory Verse

"A man's life consisteth not in the abundance of the things which he possesseth."—Luke 12:15

CUCKOO

WHO DOESN'T like a cuckoo clock? The answer is nobody. At least everybody I know gets a pleasant thrill out of seeing the little door open and the little bird come out and announce the time of day.

Not long ago newspapers told the story of an Indian who owned a little farm. The oil people discovered oil on his farm and the Indian became a millionaire in a short while. Now it seems that this Indian had always wanted a cuckoo clock, so he went to a store to buy one. And what do you think he did? He bought sixty of them instead of just one. Then he put them all in one room and had them set so that one would sound off every minute of the hour. In that way he heard a cuckoo every minute of the day. I do not know how it all turned out, but I imagine that the Indian had enough of it after an hour or two—or else became "cuckoo" himself.

The Indian made the mistake of trying to spend his money selfishly. Think how much better it would have been to have bought himself one cuckoo clock, and then have given fifty-nine to poor families that couldn't afford them. Don't you think he would have enjoyed his own cuckoo clock more if he knew that he was bringing happiness to many other homes at the same time?

In this world there are many people who have an abundance of this world's goods and who think only of themselves and their own pleasure. About the only studying some rich people do is to study ways of spending money on themselves, and so they buy yachts, and shiny limousines, and mansions, and jewels, and expensive clothes. And all the while, like the rich man in one of Jesus' parables, paying no attention to the starving and suffering people lying at their very gates.

It is a wonderful thing to have plenty of this world's goods, that is if we use it to God's glory and to make others happy.

Memory Verse

"Take heed, and beware of covetousness."—Luke 12:15

SOME PEOPLE LIKE THE DARKNESS

As A RULE, more people are afraid of the dark than the light. But some people seem to prefer darkness. Let me tell a little story that will help you understand what I mean. All of you have heard of the great poet Oliver Wendell Holmes. Well, one day he was walking across a field, and as he did so he saw a large, flat stone. For no particular reason he took a notion to overturn the stone. Then he saw hundreds of little bugs and worms—fifty-seven varieties of them. There were big ones and little ones, fuzzy ones and shiny ones, fast ones and slow ones, bugs with long legs and short legs, four legs and a thousand legs, and some with no legs. While all these bugs and worms were different in appearance, they did have one thing in common—they all scampered for holes in the ground, or places to hide under the stones and the dirt. They didn't like the light.

And that's the way it is with bad people in the human world. They prefer the darkness. Have you ever noticed that most crimes are committed at night? That's when thieves and robbers do their evil work. That's when bad men are on the prowl. And it isn't only the men; some bad women love the darkness too. All kinds of sin thrive at night. That is when the taverns are doing their biggest business. Every day newspapers tell us about the bad things that happened the night before. Yes, some human beings are not much better than bugs and vermin—at least they love the darkness rather than the light. They think the darkness will hide their evil deeds.

Real Christian people love the light. The Bible is a lamp to enlighten us. The church teaches us to be open-faced, honest, truthful, pure in heart. Jesus taught us to let our light shine, not hide it under a bushel.

Memory Verse

"Men loved darkness rather than light, because their deeds were evil."—John 3:19

HOW THE ROSE KEPT FRESH

ONE OF the greatest doctors who ever lived in Baltimore, Maryland, was Howard A. Kelly. People from all over the world came to him for help, and the lives of thousands were saved or prolonged because of his skill and devotion to duty.

Although he was a very busy man, he never allowed his duties as a physician and surgeon to interfere with his duties as a Christian. Not only was he in his place in church every Sunday, but it was his custom to read the Bible every morning before breakfast, sometimes for as long as an hour. Dr. Kelly believed and taught that the sabbath was a holy day and should be kept for holy purposes. He belonged to the Pocket Testament League and made many public speeches in which he urged men and women to carry copies of the New Testament in their pockets or their pocketbooks.

But what I want to tell you about is Dr. Kelly's famous rose. He loved flowers, and wherever he went he usually had a beautiful rose on his coat lapel. One thing puzzled his fellow doctors and other friends—how did that rose stay fresh so long? Instead of wilting in an hour or two, his rose stayed fresh all day. One day, with twinkling eyes, he let them have his secret. Under his lapel he had taped a little vial, or pill bottle, filled with water. Through the cork he had bored a little hole. He had put the stem of the rose through his buttonhole and into the vial of water, and that is how the rose stayed fresh.

After revealing his secret, the good doctor told his friends that this was also the secret of a beautiful and flourishing spiritual life. As Christians, we must send our roots down to the hidden springs, down to the fountain of living water. Any Christian who does not keep in touch with Christ, the water of life, will soon cease to be a Christian. Are we keeping our lives beautiful and fresh by constant contact with Jesus Christ?

Memory Verse

"Whosoever drinketh of the water that I shall give him shall never thirst."—John 4:14

THREE INDIAN BOYS

THERE IS an old Indian story that tells about an Indian chief and his three sons. The boys were growing into young manhood, so the old chief took them out one day to a high hill and pointed to a mountain in the distance. "Go," said he, "climb as high up that mountain as you can and bring back a memento of your adventure."

So the boys set out for the mountain. Several days passed by and one of the boys returned. "Father," he said, "I climbed so high up that mountain that there was hardly anything growing where I stopped. I brought back a most unusual flower that does not grow down here in the valley." The next day another son returned. He had climbed far beyond the line of vegetation where it was so cold and stormy that trees and shrubbery could not grow. With him he brought as a trophy a peculiar stone he had picked from the mountain slope. The following day the third son returned. His face was all aglow and there was a sparkle in his eyes as he said, "Father, I climbed to the top of the mountain and didn't bring anything back, *but I saw the sea.*" He had brought something back after all, but it wasn't in his hand; it was in his mind and heart. He had caught a vision of the great world out yonder. From that time he had a broader idea of the immensity of the world the Great Spirit had created.

All of us, old and young, should try to get broader views of the world. Many people live in a small world with themselves at the center. They are unmindful of the teeming millions who live over the horizon. To get this broad view it is no longer necessary to set out from home and climb a barren mountain. In these days of wonderful books, public libraries, good schools, mission study in our churches, and what we may read in our church periodicals we have no excuse for lacking a world vision.

Which of the three Indian boys brought back the most from the mountain? All of us agree it was the one with the vision of the sea and the world over the horizon. Boys and girls, climb that mountain and don't stop climbing until you have caught a vision of God's great world and the people in it.

Memory Verse

"Lift up your eyes and look."—John 4:35

DEAD-END STREETS

MOST EVERYBODY knows what a dead-end street is. It is a street that is closed at one end. You can't go on through, but you must turn around to get out, or you must back out. Nearly every town has some of these dead-end streets. Some are in the finest sections of our cities.

But we are not interested in the dead-end streets of any particular city this morning. I want to tell you of some dead-end streets of another kind.

The first we shall call "Disobedience Street." Boys and girls who do not obey their parents, men and women who do not respect authority, or the law, or the teachings of God, are on this street, which has a dead end. Sooner or later people who travel this way get to the end, and too often they find it impossible to turn around or to back out.

Another street with a dead end we shall call "Bluff Street." Those who travel on this street are trying to get through life by putting up a bluff. They are insincere. They just pretend. There is nothing back of them. Such people seem to get along well for a while, but at last they get to the end and can go no farther.

"Falsehood Street" has a dead end. It gets you nowhere. In fact, it does get you somewhere, but that somewhere is trouble. A man once said with a smile, "A lie is a very present help in trouble." What he should have said was, "A lie is a sure way into trouble." This is a dangerous street to travel. All sorts of bad characters loiter here. And when you get to the end of the street, if you get that far, you will find it very hard to get out of the difficulties in which you find yourself.

The fourth street we shall call "Dishonesty Street." A surprising number of people think this street is a short cut to getting rich, or getting by with little effort. "Dishonesty Street" is a short street. You get to the end before you realize it. Any sensible person will tell you that.

A PICTURE OF PEACE

IF YOU children were art students and the teacher should tell you to draw pictures that would suggest peace, what would you draw? Perhaps one of you would draw a picture of a field with sheep peacefully grazing; maybe another would draw a picture of a lake with not a ripple on the surface; and another might draw a picture of soldiers from enemy armies smiling at each other and shaking hands.

A famous artist once painted a picture he named "Peace." At first glance it seemed to suggest everything else but peace. An awful storm was in progress. There were black clouds and sharp lightning. It must have been thundering too, but the artist couldn't put that on the canvas. The trees were bent over from the strong wind, and the rain was coming down in torrents. Near by was a body of water and the waves were whipped into a fury by the storm. And yet the artist called his picture "Peace."

Now I will tell you why. Nestled under a shelf of rock, far up on a cliff, sat several little birds. They were sheltered from both the wind and the rain. They knew they were safe and they were at peace. There were no signs of excitement or distress; all was serene with them. The little birds had learned to trust their heavenly Father, so they were sitting out the storm.

The world in which we live is a stormy world. There is so much trouble and sorrow, so much of gloom and doubt. The dark war clouds seem never to leave the skies. Some people are ready to believe there is no such thing as peace. Yet some Christians have learned to trust God just as did those little birds under the cliff. God will help us have quiet hearts and serene minds no matter how

81

terrible the tempests that sweep across the world. Let us all try to have the peace of God in our hearts no matter how stormy life may become.

Memory Verse

"My peace I give unto you. . . . Let not your heart be troubled, neither let it be afraid."—John 14:27

LIVING THE CHRISTIAN WAY

SOMETIME AGO a high school conducted a popularity contest. All the students were given ballots and they voted on the most popular boy and girl, the best dressed, the best looking, the best athlete, the most studious, the one with the best personality, the one most likely to make good, and the best Christian character.

Who do you think won the honor of being voted the best Christian character? It was a Jewish boy who didn't even consider himself a Christian. I imagine there were a lot of red faces among the Gentile boys and girls who belonged to the various churches in that town.

This is how the Jewish boy came to be voted that honor. The students in their voting didn't pay any attention to race, or family history, or church connection. They thought only of Christian virtues or qualities they saw in the lives of the other students. This Jewish boy was judged to have more Christlike qualities than any of the rest. He was humble, kind, gentle in his manners, unselfish, peace-loving, friendly, studious, followed the Golden Rule, was sincere, honest, truthful, and was always going about doing good. His life, more than that of all the others, reminded the students of Christ.

The students probably made a mistake in calling him a Christian character if he didn't accept Christ as his Savior and Lord. On the other hand, the lad had about the highest compliment paid to him that was possible for the students to award.

After all, Jesus was not so much concerned with getting people to join the church, and have their names enrolled on the church books, as he was to have them live according to his teachings, and according to God's will.

THE $50,000 VIOLIN

IT IS said that once a great violinist was advertised to give a concert on a violin that had cost $50,000. Of course a lot of people went to hear his performance. When the time arrived, out stepped the musician, made a bow, and started to play. When he completed his first number the people applauded with much clapping and cheers, demanding an encore. Well, what do you think the violinist did? He took his violin by the handle and deliberately smashed it into splinters on the back of a chair. An awful hush came over the audience. They thought the musician had lost his mind. Then with a smile the artist said, "Ladies and gentlemen, the violin I smashed was bought at a secondhand shop this afternoon for $2.00. I shall now play on the $50,000 violin."

Well, what does this prove? It proves that if you have ability, if you "have the goods," as we sometimes say, the lack of equipment will not hold you down. An organist was in great demand for concert work. In an interview he said that when he was a boy, to get started in music he took an ordinary board and made a diagram of a piano keyboard. Someone helped him learn the scales, and he would practice "music" on a board that couldn't give one musical sound. In this way he became familiar with the piano keyboard, and after a while his chance came and he was ready.

It has been said that the simplest form of a university is a good teacher on one end of a log and an eager student on the other end.

Equipment has its great value, of course, but lacking such advantages, many boys and girls have succeeded anyway. So, boys and girls, don't sit around and wait for Old Man Opportunity to come your way. Go out and hunt him up. "Do the best you can, where you are, with what you have."

Memory Verse

"Such as I have give I thee."—Acts **3:6**

TONY'S TALENT

About THREE hundred years ago three boys in Cremona, Italy, were pals. One of them was named Antonio, but everybody nicknamed him Tony. Now it seems that Tony's pals were talented boys, while Tony didn't seem to be talented at all. When they went to parties they could sing and play musical instruments, but poor Tony had to sit back while the others "stole the show."

But even though Tony couldn't sing or play a musical instrument, he wasn't completely without talents, either. He enjoyed whittling with his pocketknife. He knew a lot about wood, and he had a lot of patience. So what do you think Tony did? He made a violin. Tony thought to himself, "If I can't make music, maybe I can make a musical instrument." So he carefully selected the wood, sharpened his knife, and whittled away. He sandpapered and polished and glued, and whatever else had to be done, and then one day he showed his violin to his friends. They were so amazed at its wonderful tones that they urged him to show it to the greatest musicians of his day, and they all pronounced it the best violin they had ever played or heard. So Tony went to making violins, and if you ask anybody who plays a violin, whose violins are the best in the world, you will learn it was Antonio Stradivari. To own one of these famous violins is perhaps the greatest desire in the hearts of all who play this instrument.

Now suppose Tony had sulked in a corner just because he had no special musical talent—he couldn't sing or play. Well, the other two boys are forgotten, while the name of Antonio Stradivari will live as long as the world endures. Jesus taught us that some have one kind of talent, some have another kind, but whatever our talent may be, we should use it to the glory of God. If we ask God for help, he will reveal to us what our special talents are and help us to develop them. Remember, it is not always those who are "the life of the party" who are most successful in later life.

Memory Verse

"Lord, what wilt thou have me to do?"—Acts 9:6

THE LEGEND OF THE LILIES

THERE IS a beautiful old legend that has come down through the ages to the effect that after Jesus had come forth from the tomb, and walked in Joseph's garden, white lilies grew in his footprints in the earth. It is just a legend, of course, but it teaches us a great truth just the same.

Wherever Jesus has been, beauty has followed as a matter of course. A missionary once said he could tell as soon as he entered an African jungle village if any other missionary had ever been there before. If Jesus had been preached to the people, there were sure to be some evidences of it in their lives and characters, and even in the village itself. Wherever Jesus has walked, he has left behind him a trail of beautiful things such as love, joy, peace, kindness, truth, honesty, purity, reverence.

A Christian doctor retired at an early age in order to devote his time fully to charitable work in the slums of a great city. A newspaper reporter called at his home to interview him but found him out. The doctor's wife said the reporter might find him in a certain tenement that morning. "How will I recognize him?" asked the reporter. "Oh, just look for a man who will be helping someone," said the doctor's wife. So it was with Jesus. The Bible tells us that Jesus "went about doing good." He didn't have office hours and demand that people come to him for help. He went where they were and sought to relieve their sorrows and sufferings.

Should it not be so with all who claim to be followers of Christ? If we do his will, we shall leave behind us, as we go about, a trail of beautiful words and deeds, just as the legend says lilies grew in the footprints of Jesus.

Memory Verse

"Jesus . . . went about doing good."—Acts 10:38

WHAT DID YOU GET?

SOME BOYS and girls never get inside a church and do not know what a church service is like. One such little boy went to visit his uncle in the country, and when Sunday came, the uncle and his family all went to the village church, taking the little boy along. On their way home the uncle asked his little nephew how he liked the church service. "Just fine," said the little fellow. "I liked the nice music, the nice people, and the Sunday-school teacher, and the boys and girls, and the preacher. And wasn't it nice of those men to pass plates of money around? I got 85 cents, Uncle. What did you get?" Of course, the uncle was very much ashamed that his little nephew had not understood the meaning of the offering, and had taken money from the plate. They turned around and went to the church, returned the money, and explained the misunderstanding. The little boy was not to be blamed because no one had ever told him about the Christian grace of giving; how it requires money to carry on the Lord's work at home and abroad.

Do you know, children, that some grown-up folk have about the same idea of the church? They think it is a place to get something.

We are supposed to get something there, of course, but first of all the church is a place where we give something. We give God our worship, our love, our talents, ourselves. In and through the church we give money to carry on the work of Christ's kingdom in the world. But some people insist on going to church to get. If they don't get eloquent sermons, beautiful music, a lot of friendliness, a Christmas gift, a birthday card, or an invitation to a social, they stop going to church. These things may all be a part of church life and work, yet if we are sincere and have the right motive, we will go to church not first of all to get something, but to give.

Memory Verse

"It is more blessed to give than to receive."—Acts 20:35

HE MISSED THE SHIP

A GREAT, new ship was about to leave England for New York. A man had made a reservation for passage on the ship and was on a train that was to take him to the port. The train was late and it seemed the man would miss the ship. Now the man was a Christian, and believed in prayer, so he prayed to God to help him catch the liner. Well, the train didn't get there in time, the man missed the ship, and he was terribly disappointed. In addition, it cost him a lot of money. Somehow he felt that God had been unkind to him. He felt that his prayer was unanswered. A few days later the message came that the great steamship, the "Titanic," had struck an iceberg and sixteen hundred people had gone down into the sea. Never again would that man doubt that God had answered his prayer.

You know, boys and girls, that "No" can be an answer as well as "Yes." Often our parents say "No" to us when we ask for something or other. They do it because it is for our own good. It would be a tragedy indeed if everything we asked were granted us. A little child sees a pretty bottle and cries for it. The bottle may contain poison, and so the mother puts it out of reach. It is better to let the child cry and be disappointed, even to have the child think the mother is cruel. Someday the child will be able to understand.

One of the worst things that could possibly happen to us would be to have our own way in everything, and get everything we ask for.

What we need to do is to make our desires known to God, to pray for the things we think we need and would make us happy, then be satisfied with whatever answer our heavenly Father gives. If he does not answer our prayers in just the way we think, we must remember that he knows best. He loves us and will do for us what he knows is best.

Memory Verse

"All things work together for good to them that love God."— Rom. 8:28

THEY ALL HAD A PAIN

As an old man passed along a street one day he noticed a group of children, all of them crying. Feeling that something awful must have happened, he asked one little boy, "What's the matter with all you children? What has happened?" With tearful eyes and a sobbing voice the little fellow replied, "Please, sir, we all have a pain in Billy's stomach." I hope that is a true story, and I can imagine that it is. I am sure that all little children are sorry when their little brothers, or sisters, or playmates are ill, or in trouble, and that is the way it ought to be. I wish it were more true than it is of grown-up folk. Unfortunately, many do not seem to care when others are in distress.

You have heard the parable of the good Samaritan, as given by Jesus. Someone has said that the attitude of the robbers may be expressed in these words: "What's yours is mine; I'll take it." The attitude of the hardhearted priest and Levite was: "What's mine is mine; I'll keep it." But the attitude of the kindhearted Samaritan was: "What's mine is ours; we'll share it."

Jesus taught his followers to live shared lives, to be sympathetic with the poor and the sick, to do all they could to relieve their troubles. One of the great hymns of the church, John Fawcett's "Blest be the tie that binds," very beautifully shows how Christians should enter into the joys and sorrows of each other:

> We share each other's woes,
> Each other's burdens bear,
> And often for each other flows
> The sympathizing tear.

That is what the little children were doing in the story of the children who all had a pain in Billy's stomach. They shed sympathizing tears. The world is in deep distress. Millions are suffering untold agonies of body, mind, and spirit. Millions are homeless, hungry, cold, and see nothing ahead but misery and death. We are Christians, and that means we must share their sorrows and relieve their distresses just as much as we can.

Memory Verse

"Rejoice with them that do rejoice, and weep with them that weep."—Rom. 12:15

A HANDFUL OF GOOSEBERRIES

MANY, MANY years ago a little girl reached through a neighbor's garden fence and grabbed a handful of gooseberries. No one saw her do it, and it is likely the owner of the garden wouldn't have cared a mite. Most anybody would give a little girl a handful of gooseberries if he had them to give. Twenty-five years later this girl, then happily married, sent her old neighbor twenty-five cents in a letter. She wrote what she had done as a child. The matter had been on her conscience ever since, so she wanted to pay for those berries, with interest. She said in the letter: "I know you will laugh at this; I know you will say I was welcome to the berries; but I did wrong and I'll never be happy until I confess what I did and pay for what I took."

What a wonderful world this would be if everybody was that conscientious! Now let me tell you the story of the world's most unusual diploma. On the walls of a Southern university hangs a diploma. It is just like thousands of diplomas that have been awarded students upon completion of their courses of study. It tells that on a certain date this particular student was awarded his degree and the diploma, and it is properly signed by the president and other officials. But the unusual thing about this diploma is that the name of the student has been cut out with a sharp knife. It seems that years after graduation, the student could not forget having cheated in some of the examinations. He got no pleasure out of being a graduate of the school when he had become such by dishonesty, so he returned the diploma. If all graduates who cheated in their examinations should return their diplomas, it would create quite a sensation.

Call this girl who paid for a handful of gooseberries, and this graduate who returned his diploma, cranks if you want to, but this country of ours could use a few more conscientious citizens than it now has.

Memory Verse

"Provide things honest in the sight of all men."—Rom. 12:17

HONEYBEES WITHOUT STINGS

WHEN THE good old summertime comes again, how glad that makes boys and girls. What a lot of fun it is to play out of doors without having to be bundled up, to take walks in the country or the park, to go swimming, play ball, to go on picnics, and all the other things boys and girls do in summer.

One thing we are sure to see in summer if we live near the clover fields or flower gardens is the honeybee. The honeybee is a very busy little creature and is very interesting. However, I advise you not to get too chummy with honeybees. You might be sorry. Honeybees may be ever so sweet in some ways, but many boys and girls have had the bitter experience of being stung by them.

This morning I want to tell you about some honeybees without stings. The first is "Be honest." No one has ever been sorry for having been honest. Some dishonest people think they are getting along just fine, but after a while they get caught and must pay the penalty. In other words, dishonesty leaves a sting behind. The second honeybee without a sting is "Be truthful." Here again is a "bee" that you can get close to without danger. Everybody loves this "honeybee." We love people who tell the truth. Employers want such folk. In our circle of friends we want only those who are truthful. The third "honeybee" is "Be cheerful." A great man once said, "There is a lot of unnecessary sniffling in the world." We love people who are glad and full of fun, who look on the sunny side. We shun people who are gloomy and sour, and can't enjoy a joke. The last "honeybee" I shall mention is "Be reverent." This is just another way of saying that love for God, for God's house, and God's day, and God's Book will bring no regrets. There is no sting in being reverent. Now I am going to read a little verse from the *Endeavor Times,* called "A Hive of Bees."

> B hopeful, B cheerful, B happy, B kind,
> B busy of body, B modest of mind,
> B earnest, B truthful, B firm and B fair;
> Of all Miss B Havior B sure to B-ware;
> B-think, ere you stumble, of what may B-fall;
> B true to yourself, and B faithful to all.

Memory Verse

"Be not overcome of evil, but overcome evil with good."—Rom. 12:21

THREE BOYS IN A BOAT

Rub-a-dub, dub, three men in a tub." So goes the old nursery rhyme. Well, this isn't a story about three men in a tub, but about three boys in a boat. The boat was on the Niagara River, above the falls, where the water was just beginning to become swift and dangerous. The boys knew there was danger of getting into the swift current and not being able to pull the boat to shore, but they were adventurous and inclined to "show off" because they were being watched by people on the bank of the river. The people shouted warnings, but the boys kept on playing with danger. They would let their boat drift into the rapid waters, then pull hard on the oars until they got back to safety. After a while they would do it again and again. Every time they would drift a little farther before bending their strong young backs to the oars and pulling themselves to safety.

Well, this is what happened. They allowed the boat to drift a little too far, or they became a little too tired from their exertion, and the boat drifted into the rapid waters in spite of all they could do to return to safety. Amid their own screams, and the screams of friends on the shore, the boat and the boys went over the falls and they lost their lives. And all because they thought they were strong enough to pull themselves out of danger before it was too late. Thousands of boys and girls have made that mistake with respect to sin. They felt they could trifle with sin; they made light of it; they felt they could pull themselves to safety whenever they chose; but eventually their moral strength failed, they went a little too far, and lost their souls as a result. Someone has said, "There is a hidden boundary between God's patience and his wrath." There is a point on the river of life beyond which we had better not drift. Better stay in the safe waters of the home and the church.

Memory Verse

"Let him that thinketh he standeth take heed lest he fall."—
I Cor. 10:12

BONES

THERE ARE many ways of grouping Christians. One way is by denominations. And so we have Methodists, Baptists, Roman Catholics, Lutherans, and over two hundred other denominations. Someone has said that all Christians could be put into one of three groups—"workers," "jerkers," and "shirkers." The workers are the ones who really keep the church going; the jerkers are those who take hold of the work occasionally; the shirkers are those who avoid any and all opportunities to help with the dear Lord's work.

Now here is still another way to classify Christian people: "Jawbone Christians" are the ones who talk a lot about religion, yet do very little to help the work along. They can quote scripture and make it prove almost anything. Some of this type of Christian are good at telling others what to do and what not to do, while getting off as easy as possible themselves. A young woman was called "a promising young lady." She was always promising to help with the work at the church, promising to serve, to give to the work, to attend the services. Unfortunately she did nothing much but promise.

"Wishbone Christians" are the people who wish the church well, and want it to get ahead, but they let it go at that. They wish more people would attend, but they never invite others to come; they wish people would join the church, but they never urge a soul to do it; they wish the church would have enough money for its work, but they hold back when it comes to liberal giving. Yes, every church has a lot of "wishbone Christians."

"Backbone Christians" are the faithful ones who have courage to do their duty as Christ directs. They have spunk, grit, and what it takes to make church work hum along. They don't do much talking, or sit around wishing. They say, "We've got a job to do, let's do it." Every church needs more "backbone Christians."

Memory Verse

"Though I speak with the tongues of men and of angels, and have not charity, I am become as sounding brass, or a tinkling cymbal."—I Cor. 13:1

OUR SUBSTITUTE

HAVE YOU ever been in an old-fashioned country flour mill? I doubt it, because most of them have been torn down or have fallen down. The big city mills have put the little country mills out of business. But many years ago they were a familiar sight along the country roads. The farmers brought their grain to be ground into flour and feed. It was interesting to see the big water wheel go around and around, also the big stone grinders.

Many years ago in one of these mills a little boy was playing. He had no business there and he knew it, but you know how some boys disobey. Well, this is what happened. His clothing got caught in the machinery and it was pulling him toward it, closer and closer. It seemed that nothing could prevent him from being crushed to death by the big cogwheels.

Now there worked in the mill a Negro, and he happened to see the little boy being drawn into the machinery. He didn't have time to run to the place where the machinery could be shut down. He knew the only thing to be done was to jam the wheels and make it stop. There wasn't a thing handy to put into the cogwheels, so what do you think he did? He deliberately put his elbow into the wheels and that caused the machine to stop, and the boy's life was saved. The poor man's arm was terribly crushed and mangled. The doctors had to cut it off, but he died from the effects. He gave his life to save the little boy. He was the little boy's substitute.

Isn't that just what Jesus Christ has done for every one of us? Slowly but surely we were being drawn by sin to an awful doom. Then the Lord Jesus became our substitute. He died upon the cross that we might live.

I know the little boy in the story never forgot the man who died in his place. Do we remember Jesus Christ? Do we appreciate his sufferings for us?

Memory Verse

"Christ died for our sins."—I Cor. 15:3

LIKE A BOOK

DID YOU ever hear someone say of another, "I can read him like a book?" What he means, of course, is that he can understand the other fellow very easily. Well, when you stop to think about it, people are very much like books.

Books have names, and so do we. Sometimes the names are long, sometimes they are short. Sometimes the names of books are hard to pronounce, sometimes they are easy. The name of a book doesn't always indicate what is in the book. In fact, the names of books and of people are not so important. The important thing is what is inside.

Some books are good, and some are bad. And that is the way it is with people too. Bad books, like bad people, should be shunned. Bad books, like bad people, can put evil ideas into our heads and lead into no end of trouble. We should shun evil books just as we should shun evil companions.

You can't tell what's in a book by its cover. Sometimes bookmakers, in order to make their books attractive to prospective customers, will put very fancy bindings on them, perhaps leather, and the title will be stamped in gold. In recent years they have been designing temporary paper covers that are very attractive. But just as I said about the name of the book, the important thing is what is inside. Some people who dress in elegant and fashionable clothes have very dull minds and perhaps impure hearts, and some people whose bodies are clothed in very simple and inexpensive garments have brilliant minds and hearts of gold. The old folks used to have a saying, "There's many a noble heart that beats under a faded shawl."

People read us like books. That's what I started out to say. Yes, our lives are open books to most people. The words we speak, the places we go, the attitudes we take, our likes and dislikes, help others to look right into our hearts and read what is there.

Memory Verse

"Ye are our epistle, . . . known and read of all men."—II Cor. 3:2

A BIRTHDAY PARADE

ONCE THERE was a little girl who was born on the Fourth of July. Several years later there was a big Independence Day parade in the town where she lived, and the little girl asked her mother what it was all about. The mother, not meaning to tell a fib, said with a laugh, "Why, my dear, the parade is to celebrate my little girl's birthday." For a number of years the little girl really thought the Fourth of July celebrations were in her honor.

No doubt the mother did wrong to tell the little girl what she did, or at least she was not tactful. On the other hand, there is a sense in which a Fourth of July parade belongs to every little girl and boy, and big ones too.

I wonder how many of us stop and think of the many things that are planned for our happiness. Your neighbor has beautiful roses, perhaps. They are not his alone. They belong to the neighborhood. Everybody may admire them and get a lift by just looking at them. Then there is the beautiful music we hear in the churches, concert halls, and over the radio. Those who compose the music, those who play the music, do it for our enjoyment. They would be unhappy if it did not make the people happy. And how about our city parks with their lovely landscaping, athletic fields, and perhaps a zoo? What are they for? They are to bring happiness to the people.

And what shall we say about this beautiful world in which we live? What is it for? Whom is it for? On every hand we see reminders that there is a loving God who has created all these beauties and blessings to make us happy. And this same God has given us our Savior Jesus Christ, and the church, and the holy Bible, and the Sabbath day. When we think of all our blessings, let us not forget that they are for us, each one of us.

Memory Verse

"All things are for your sakes."—II Cor. 4:15

PIGS ARE PIGS

WHAT DO you know about pigs? If you have ever lived on a
farm, or have just visited one, you know this much about pigs
—they love to wallow in the mud. Pigs are notorious for their lack of
cleanliness. Some animals seem to take pride in their appearance,
but not pigs. And when they eat, well, they eat "just like pigs."
When the farmer pours the slop into their troughs, the pigs squeal,
push each other out of the way, and often put their front feet right
into their food. This seems to be their nature.

One time, so a story goes, a city man bought a farm and wanted to
raise some pigs. When he observed their filthy habits, he thought
he would try an experiment. So he scrubbed the pigs with brushes
and soapy water until they were as clean as could be. Then his wife
brought some perfume and sprayed it on the pigs. To complete the
job they put beautiful pink ribbons around the necks of the pigs.
Surely, they thought, this will raise the self-respect of the pigs and
make them want to be pretty and clean.

When they turned the pigs loose, what do you think they did?
You guessed it. They struck out for the mud and soon were rolling
around in their old wallowing place. Water, soap, perfume, and
pink ribbons didn't change their natures. A neighbor who knew all
about pigs said to the man, with a smile: "Brother, you don't know
much about pigs. You just can't change their natures."

Some human beings live almost like pigs, and no matter how you
try, you just can't change their natures. They just like to live in
the dirt. Clean them up, perfume them, and put pink ribbons on
them, but soon they will be back in their old habits.

But it is not only the bodies and homes of people that need cleans-
ing. Our hearts by nature are unclean, and the only way they can
be set right is for us to let God change our evil natures. Education,
wealth, fashionable garments, and beauty parlors can't change our
hearts. That can be done only by the grace of God. All of us have
need to pray the prayer of the psalmist, "Create in me a clean
heart, O God."

"If any man be in Christ, he is a new creature."—II Cor. 5:17

AN INDIAN GIVER

DO YOU boys and girls know what an "Indian giver" is? When your pastor was a boy, we called people "Indian givers" if they gave something to us, then took it back. How the idea got started no one seems to know, and it certainly is not fair to the Indians. They were compelled to give the early white settlers much, and certainly they didn't get much back.

But my story has to do with a different sort of an Indian giver. A pioneer preacher was conducting a revival meeting in a Western town, and then, as now, it was necessary to pass the collection plates for the offerings of the people. When the collector passed the plate to an Indian who was in the audience, the Indian took the plate from the collector's hand, put it on the floor in the aisle, then stood upon the plate. The poor collector was so surprised he didn't know what to do next, and the entire congregation shared his astonishment. Then the Indian, as best he could, explained his act. "Me no have money," he said, "so me give myself."

Now I certainly am not suggesting that people should do the dramatic thing this Indian did. On the other hand, would it not be wonderful if all who presume to worship God would really and truly give themselves to him? Many of us have money to give, and we give it, but do we really give ourselves to Christ?

Take my silver and my gold;
Not a mite would I withhold.

The church needs gifts of silver and gold to carry on its work and to carry out the purposes of Christ, but what is most needed is the consecration of life itself. So let us really mean it when we sing the old hymn:

Take my life, and let it be
Consecrated, Lord, to thee.

Memory Verse

"Come out from among them, and be ye separate, saith the Lord."
—II Cor. 6:17

IF CHRIST HAD NOT COME

BOYS AND girls, how good are you at imagining? Suppose we try to imagine what this world would be like without any colors in it. This would mean there would be no rainbows, or sunsets, or pretty skies and clouds. The flowers wouldn't be flowers, and what would our lawns and meadows be like? We couldn't look forward to blossomtime in the spring, and the wonderful beauties of autumn. There would be no redbirds, or bluebirds, or yellow canaries. All the girls' dresses would look alike, and when Christmas came around, there would be no use for the colored ornaments and lights. It wouldn't be very nice in this world if we did not have the colors God has given us, do you think?

Well, boys and girls, now try to imagine what it would be like to live in your town if Jesus Christ were not known or loved there. To start with, there would be no churches, and if there were no churches, there would be no churchgoing; and if there were no churchgoing, soon there would be no Christians, and if there were no Christians, soon the town would be turned over to wicked people.

If there were no churches and no Christians, there would be no Christmas. How would you like that?

And if there were no churches, soon we would be without hospitals, and orphanages, and old folks' homes, and people who like to help those who sorrow and suffer.

Yes, this would be a gloomy, unattractive old world without colors, and even gloomier and less attractive without Jesus Christ. Have we ever thanked God for the beautiful colors, and for our eyes with which we see them? And have we ever thanked God for Jesus Christ, who brought so many wonderful blessings with him into the world?

Memory Verse

"Thanks be unto God for his unspeakable gift."—II Cor. 9:15

PULLING THE CHURCH UPHILL

WE LOVE to think of the United States as a land of templed hills. This is because in almost every community there is a church, and many of our churches are built on hills or high places. There is something very inspiring about a church built on a hill, with a steeple like a finger pointing to the sky.

The story is told of a little church that was built at the bottom of a hill. As the years passed, the church prospered and the people were sorry the church had not been built on top of the hill. Now it seems that the pastor had imagination. One day he came up with this idea. He said: "Let us raise the church, put it on wheels, and pull it to a new foundation on top of the hill." The people agreed, and the day came for all the members to come and help pull the church up the hill. The pastor took hold of the long rope, then the official members, and everybody else who was willing. All together they pulled, and the church started on its journey. It was lots of fun—for a while. Then the people began to get a little tired. One after another let go the rope, and the church moved slower and slower. Imagine the surprise and discouragement of the pastor and officials when they looked around and saw what was happening.

I do not know the rest of the story, but I hope the people rallied and that the church finally got to the top of the hill.

That is the way it is with church work. Too often the people leave it to the pastor and official board to do all the pulling. They can do just so much, no more. They need the help of everybody, old and young alike.

The coach in a tug of war always tells the athletes, "It isn't the sudden and occasional jerks that count, but the steady pull."

Do you want your church to "go places"? Do you want it to go up-hill? Then get hold of the rope and pull steadily.

Memory Verse

"Let us not be weary in well doing."—Gal. 6:9

LISTEN TO WHAT THE POSTAGE STAMP SAYS

IT IS doubtful if anything in the world has gone as many places, seen as many sights, and had as many adventures as the postage stamp. What wonderful stories it could tell us if it could speak!

Here is some of the advice I think the postage stamp would give boys and girls if it could speak:

"Be useful." The postage stamp adds a bit of color and ornamentation to the envelope, but that isn't the big idea. It serves a very useful purpose. It has a job to do, and does it well.

"Stick to your job." The stamp doesn't stop work until its mission is completed. It has no rest day nor night until it delivers the letter we entrust with it. Some of us could learn a lesson from the postage stamp and stick to our jobs a little better than we do.

"Take your licking." The postage stamp has to have at least one good licking. Most boys and girls have profited by a good "licking" now and then. I remember some "lickings" that did me a lot of good although I was not enthusiastic for them at the time.

"Don't mind being smeared." Being smeared is all part of a postage stamp's life. The postal clerks see to it that every one gets some black ink daubed on it. Very few boys and girls ever grow up without having some fibs told about them, or ugly things said about them. Especially if you get into public life is this true. But like the postage stamp, we must take it all as a matter of course. It serves a purpose in the end.

"Think of great persons and great events." I know each of you has often looked at the pictures on the stamps, pictures of George Washington, Thomas Jefferson, Abraham Lincoln, and many other great Americans. One of my most prized stamps shows the four brave chaplains who gave their lifebelts to others and then went down with their torpedoed ship. If stamps can remind people of great persons, then our lives ought to remind people of Jesus Christ, whose image we should bear.

Memory Verse

"I bear in my body the marks of the Lord Jesus."—Gal. 6:17

TRACKS IN THE SNOW

WHO DOESN'T like to make tracks in the snow? And it isn't only boys and girls. A lot of grownups enjoy plodding in the snow, at least until they get out of breath.

Two little boys were enjoying the first heavy snowfall of the winter. They threw snowballs, made several snowmen, and rolled a big snowball until it was so large they couldn't push it any longer. Then one of the boys said, "Let's see who can make the straightest tracks across that field." So over the fence they went and started across the field. When they got to the other side of the field and looked back, it was seen that one boy made an almost straight path across the field, while the other boy's tracks were zigzagged.

I wonder if any boy or girl here can tell me the secret why one boy's tracks were so straight? The answer was given by the boy himself. He said, "I picked out a certain post on the other side of the field and kept my eyes on it, always walking straight toward it." That was the secret of the straight path. The other boy had looked down or around, and the result was that he wandered in all directions.

Walking on the straight pathway through life is pretty much like making a pathway through the snow. We need to have a goal. We need to fix our eyes on something or somebody. Jesus Christ is the one upon whom to fix our eyes as we journey through life. If we keep looking to him, we shall make a straight path. If we look down or around us, we are certain to go astray.

There's another thing about having a goal as we journey through life. We don't have to cover as much ground. When a boy and a dog go for a walk, the dog will probably cover twice as much ground as the boy because the dog will be running this way and that way, zigzagging all the while. Yes, it's easiest and best in the end to keep on the straight and narrow pathway that leads to heaven.

Memory Verse

"I press toward the mark for the prize of the high calling of God in Christ Jesus."—Phil. 3:14

THREE DRINKS--THREE MURDERS

HOW WOULD you boys and girls like a little history lesson? Some of the things I am going to tell you are in the history books you will study at school. A few things I shall tell you are not found in the books. For some reason those who choose our textbooks don't like to inform us of the doings of King Alcohol.

On the night of April 14, 1865, a man went into a saloon in Washington for a glass of strong liquor. He drank it, then went straight to Ford's Theater, where President Abraham Lincoln was enjoying a play, and fired the shot that killed the great President. The guard who was supposed to be on duty near the President had slipped down the street for a glass of booze.

On July 2, 1881, another man went into a saloon and drank just one glass of strong drink. Then he sneaked up behind another President of the United States, James A. Garfield, and shot him in the back.

The third of our martyred presidents was William McKinley. On September 6, 1901, a man took a drink of liquor and went immediately to where he knew the President was shaking hands with the people, and shot him.

Here were three noble Presidents, men of great value to our beloved country, who lost their lives because three other men chose to drink intoxicating liquor. And at the same time three men became murderers, resulting in their being put to death as punishment and the bringing of sorrow and disgrace to their families and friends.

Three drinks, three Presidents murdered, three men became murderers! Now multiply that by tens of thousands and you will realize the awful results of strong drink in our country.

I trust that when you children grow up, you will be so disgusted with the traffic in strong drink that you will pass laws to get rid of it, and elect men to office who will see that the laws are enforced.

Memory Verse

"Touch not; taste not; handle not."—Col. 2:21

LOOK UP!

A LAD WAS walking along the street one day when he happened to see on the ground before him a two-dollar bill. Someone had lost it, and it was his good luck to find it. But it turned out to be bad luck in the end. From that day on, the boy always kept his eyes looking toward the ground, hoping to find another two-dollar bill, or something else of value.

Twenty-five years passed by and the man had collected a cigar box full of pins, buttons, a number of small coins, and a variety of things that had fallen by the wayside. Perhaps these things were worth picking up, but not when one considers what happened to the man himself. From stooping over so much he became a hunch back and developed trouble with his lungs. But even worse than that, the poor fellow in looking for things of little value missed finding things of much greater value. He missed the smiles of his neighbors and the beauty of the world about him—the skies, the landscapes, the birds, and the flowers.

Always looking downward toward the pavement, the poor fellow fell into the bad habit of looking downward in other ways. He became a grouch, a pessimist, an "old meany." His relatives had little respect for him, his neighbors shunned him, little children were afraid of him, and he couldn't hold a job very long. His health became poor and he went to his grave a wretched and miserable man.

How much better it would have been had he gone through life with his chin up, looking at the skies, and the stars, and into the friendly eyes of people as they passed by! Had he done so, the values that would have enriched his life would have been far greater than the two-dollar bill, the box of pins, buttons, and whatever else he found on the ground.

In one of the songs we love to sing a good motto is suggested: "I would look up, and laugh, and love, and lift." Boys and girls, that is the way to go through life.

Memory Verse

"Set your affection on things above, not on things on the earth."
—Col. 3:2

A PIN PREACHES A SERMON

Do YOU see what I have in my hand? Perhaps it is too small to be seen from where you are. It is just an ordinary pin, such as dad uses to pin a rose on his coat lapel. What do you think this pin would say if it could talk? Let us try to imagine some of the things it might say to you boys and girls.

"Be straight." Who wants a crooked pin? Nobody. Once it is bent we throw it away. Who wants crooked people around? Nobody. We don't like crooked people who tell untruths, are dishonest, and live impure lives. So the pin advises all of us, old and young, "Be straight."

"Be shiny." Who wants a rusty pin? Nobody. And nobody wants dull and gloomy folk around. The world is gloomy enough with all the ignorance and sin there is in it, so we need the brightness and sunshine of Christ reflected in the faces of his followers. Jesus said, "Let your light so shine."

"Use your head." This is something else the pin advises boys and girls. Were it not for the pin's head, we would injure our fingers when we press it into cloth, and the pin would go too far. If more people used their heads—that is, if they would think—they would be better off, and the world would be better off. Most of the trouble in the world is caused by people who don't "use their heads."

"Have a purpose in life." The pin has a point and a purpose. Many years ago there lived a young man named Daniel, who became a great leader. One little verse in the Bible gives the secret of his success—"Daniel purposed in his heart." There was point and purpose in his life. He didn't drift around from one thing to another. He knew where he was going and how to get there.

Now maybe the pin would have something else to say, but this is all the time we have. Remember what the pin has said: "Be straight, be shiny, use your head, and have a purpose in life."

Memory Verse

"Hold fast that which is good."—I Thess. 5:21

THE LAZY OX

THE CHARACTERS in our story are an ox, a mule, a farmer, and a butcher. There is an old legend that a farmer often yoked an ox and a mule together for plowing and other work on his farm. The ox was lazy, but the mule was quite willing to do his duty. One night the ox and mule were together in the barn when the ox said to the mule, "Let's play a trick on the old man tomorrow and pretend we are sick." The mule refused, but the ox decided to try it by himself. So the next day the farmer had to get along with only the mule to help him. At night the ox asked the mule, "What did the old man say?" "Nothing," replied the mule. Thinking his plan was working pretty well, the ox tried it the second day, and a third, and a fourth. Each evening the ox would ask the mule what the farmer had said about it, and each evening the mule would reply "Nothing." Then one evening the mule said to the ox, "The farmer didn't say anything about you not working today, but I saw him have a long talk with the butcher."

If the ox didn't want to work, the farmer thought he might just as well turn him over to the butcher.

Nobody likes lazy people and we don't want to have them around. Someone has said that the lazy man "is the last man hired and the first man fired." Sometimes employers do not know their workers are lazy until after they are hired, but if they are found to be lazy, you may be sure they will be discharged as soon as possible.

The reason a lot of people do not succeed in the world is because they are just plain lazy. It isn't because they are lacking in ability, education, or health, but are trying to get by without effort.

Remember the old saying, "Any dead fish can float downstream, but it takes a live one to swim upstream." And here's another good motto, "If you itch for success, keep on scratching."

Memory Verse

"This we commanded you, that if any would not work, neither should he eat."—II Thess. 3:10

GOD'S ALARM CLOCK

PERHAPS EVERY one of you boys and girls has an alarm clock at home. You know very well what it is, and what it is for. I have a big one that makes so much noise when it goes off that it frightens me and wakes the whole neighborhood. Whenever I want the alarm to go off in the morning, I set it at night, then I wake up too early and lie awake so as to turn it off just before it rings. That doesn't make sense, does it? A lot of things don't make sense these days.

A boy named Ralph was a sleepyhead. Sometimes when his alarm clock sounded, he would reach out from his bed, turn it off, and go back to sleep. It got to be a habit with him, and after a while he became so accustomed to it that he didn't even hear it. The clock would just run down and Ralph would sleep on and on. So the clock was of no value. Now Ralph had another alarm clock. It was deep down inside him and it was called "conscience." Whenever Ralph was tempted to do wrong, his conscience would sound the alarm. Little by little Ralph got into the habit of paying no attention to his "conscience alarm clock." He cheated in school; he told some little lies, then some bigger ones; and after a while he started taking things that didn't belong to him. God's alarm clock, the conscience, kept trying to wake Ralph up to the fact that he was doing wrong, but Ralph paid no attention to it. Then one day when Ralph was a big boy, he and some other bad boys robbed a store and had to go to jail. And all because he got into the habit of paying no attention to God's alarm clock, the conscience. When George Washington was a schoolboy, he wrote in his copybook, "Labor to keep alive in your breast that little spark of celestial fire—conscience."

Memory Verse

"Holding faith, and a good conscience."—I Tim. 1:19

DON'T LET YOURSELF GO

THE STORY is told of a very wicked man who was known as an infidel. He made his will, and when he died, the lawyers read what he wanted done with his property. They discovered a very unusual bequest. He had written, "I want my farm to go to the devil." It was his way of saying he hated churches, and Christian people, and everything that Christians hold dear.

Well, the lawyers and judges went into a huddle, as we say, and tried to figure out what the law would allow them to do with the farm. The case was dragged out through the courts over several years, and in the meanwhile, what do you think happened to the farm? It went to the devil. Let me tell you what I mean.

The once-fertile fields grew up in briars; the roofs of the buildings were neglected and began to leak, then caved in, and the inside of the buildings rotted; in came owls, bats, squirrels and polecats; the well of water became filled with filth and was unfit to drink; the shutters fell off the house; and bad boys broke the windows with stones. The best way of saying what happened to the farm was, "It went to the devil." The rest of the story I do not know, but I hope the lawyers finally turned it over to some good people who took it away from the devil and reclaimed it.

Every boy and girl should be able to see the lesson in this story. If we neglect our spiritual lives, we soon go to the devil. When we neglect God, the church, our Bibles, prayer, and Christian service we soon are on the way to an unhappy end.

All of us know how important it is to take care of our health, our appearance, and our financial affairs. Is it not even more important to give good care to our souls? Remember, if we neglect our souls, old Satan will get us by and by.

Memory Verse

"Neglect not the gift that is in thee."—I Tim. 4:14

THE EASIEST THING IN THE WORLD

GUESS WHAT is the easiest thing in the world! The easiest thing I know of is to drift. You don't need to do anything, just let yourself go. Imagine you are in a boat out on a river and you want to go downstream. All you need to do is do nothing. Just put the oars in the boat and drift. The current will take you down.

Of course if you want to go upstream, or across the stream, that is something else. You can't take it easy. You must bend your back to the oars and pull hard. "Easy does it" may be a good slogan when applied to some things, but it is a poor slogan for those who would go places and do things in a Christian way. It has been said, "There are no elevators in the House of Success; you must toil up the steps, one at a time."

Another word for drifting is neglect. It too is so easy, and it always takes you down, down, down. When a farmer neglects his farm, it becomes what we call "run down." Neglect never builds up anything; it always tears down.

A lot of Christians are drifting downstream. They are not working for Christ, not putting forth any effort, not interested in making spiritual progress, and so they are slowly drifting down to an awful ending of their lives. When we neglect God and the things of God —his sabbath, his Book, his house, and his people—and neglect to pray, we are surely drifting down the stream of time to destruction.

Boys and girls, don't drift. Don't drift away from Sunday school and church, for that usually means drifting away from God and from heaven.

Memory Verse

"Therefore we ought to give the more earnest heed to the things which we have heard, lest at any time we should let them slip."— Heb. 2:1

STANDARDS

Do YOU boys and girls know what we mean by standards? Well, when you go to the store for Mother and buy some meat or some sugar, the grocer weighs it on his scales. Our system of weights is standardized, which means that a pound is a pound and an ounce is an ounce everywhere, at least in our own country. The carpenter has to have standards, or the lines of the building he builds would be crooked and ugly. His standards are the square, compass, level, plumbline, and tape measure. Our clocks have standard time, excepting when we have daylight-saving time, and this causes a lot of confusion. And so we could go on and mention the need of standards with money, education, electrical things, plumbing, automobiles, and what not. Our laws, too, are standards and we ought to respect them.

Did you ever think of the awful confusion we would have if there were no standards? Suppose there were no laws or regulations, no yardsticks or weighing scales, no clocks, no schedules, and no recipes for food! I am sure this would be a very topsy-turvy world without standards.

Maybe that is what is wrong with the world. We have not observed the standards given to us in the holy Bible. You should know that there are standards in religion and morals as well as in commerce and industry. Yet the world does just about what it pleases, paying but little heed to the laws, rules, principles, and ideals given us in God's Word.

Some of these standards given in the Bible are the Ten Commandments, the Beatitudes, the Sermon on the Mount, and the Golden Rule. What a wonderful world this would be if everybody lived by these standards! There would be no wars, no greed, no murders, no breaking up of homes, no jails, no drunkenness, no stealing, no lying, and no hate in the hearts of men.

The great standard for us all is Jesus Christ. We can never be so good, so pure, so straight, so strong, so true as he, but it is our duty to try. Should we not all do our best to live according to the pattern revealed to us by Jesus?

Memory Verse

"Let us go on unto perfection."—Heb. 6:1

LIKE AN ANGEL

IN THE public square of an Italian city a little slum girl found her only place to romp and play in the out-of-doors. With other little children of her type she played catchers, hide-and-seek, and whatever other games the children of that place played. Then one day the people of that city erected a large memorial monument in the center of the square. On a great stone pedestal stood a group of figures in marble, one of them being an angel. The little girl continued to play in the open spaces of the public square, and she found increasing delight in standing near the statue of the angel, gazing upon it with worshipful admiration.

The little girl's parents were what we call "good-for-nothing." They took no pride in themselves, their home, or their children. The home was untidy, and the children roamed the streets in filthy clothing, their hair uncombed, their faces dirty. Such children usually grow up to be problems for the community, having low ideals and bad morals.

But the little girl of our story, after gazing lovingly at the statue of the angel, ran home and washed her face, then she tried to fix her hair as she remembered the hair of the angel. Day after day she would stand before the statue, then go home to try to be more and more like that angel. Some Christian people took an interest in her and told her the story of Christ, of the need for purity in heart, as well as beauty of face and form.

As the little girl grew into womanhood she became a noble Christian, a worker among the poor and sinful people of the slums, and the people compared her with the angel in the public square. The big difference was that she was alive, and went about doing good.

Now not many of us can be inspired by the beauty of an angel of stone, but all of us know the wonderful story of the perfect life of Jesus Christ. Should we not all strive to be like him?

Memory Verse

"Looking unto Jesus the author and finisher of our faith."—Heb. 12:2

COURTESY PAYS

SOMEONE HERE has a brand-new silver dollar and will give it to the tenth person who shakes hands with him or her." That is what the chairman said at the social. Then everybody scampered around shaking hands with everybody else, each hoping to get that dollar. After a bit, someone got the dollar, but everybody else got fun out of it and became better acquainted with the others.

A few years ago some little children were playing on a pavement in a crowded section of Chicago. Along came a shabbily dressed stranger who asked the children if they knew where Mr. So-and-so lived. Most of the children just said they didn't know and went on playing. But one little girl said, "I'll ask my mother." She went inside and asked her mother, who didn't know either. Then she said, "Let me run into the grocery store and ask them." The grocer didn't know the person whose address was wanted. Then the little girl scampered up some steps to ask other people, but no one seemed to know anybody by that name. "I'm very sorry," she said to the stranger, "but it doesn't seem that anybody by that name lives in this neighborhood." "You don't need to be sorry," said the stranger, "for I have been sent out by my newspaper to give fifty dollars to the most polite person I meet today, and you are that person." So he gave the little girl the money, then he went back to his newspaper to write the story for the next day's papers. It seems the newspaper had a campaign on to encourage people to be more courteous and polite, and this was a stunt to help with the campaign. No doubt that little girl was very glad she had been so courteous, and maybe the other little girls wish they had been so too.

Courtesy may not always bring pay in money, but it is always worth while. Courtesy and kindness go along together. They are qualities everybody should have. None of us can be good Christians without them.

Memory Verse

"Be not forgetful to entertain strangers: for thereby some have entertained angels unawares."—Heb. 13:2

THE SIN OF DISCONTENT

SOMETIMES CARTOONS in magazines teach good lessons, in addition to making us laugh. For instance, I once saw a drawing of a country landscape. There were two fields divided by a fence. Each field was about the same size, and each had plenty of the same kind of grass. In each field there was a mule, and each mule had his head through the fence eating grass from the other mule's pasture. All around the mule in his own field was plenty of grass, yet the grass in the other field seemed greener or fresher, just because it was hard to get. The artist put just one word at the bottom of the picture, "Discontent."

How like mules some of us are! So often we are discontented with what we have, although we have plenty. Like those mules, we think we should be very happy if we could have what others have, while unmindful of the fact that we may already have as much or more than they.

Here's a little verse that helps us see the foolishness and sinfulness of discontent:

114

As a rule a man's a fool;
When it's hot, he wants it cool;
When it's cool, he wants it hot;
Always wanting what is not.

This sin of discontent is the mother of many other sins—covetousness, theft, meanness, selfishness, impatience, and broken homes. It makes one ill-tempered and unhappy; it takes all the joy out of life for you and for everybody about you.

Let us make very sure that we are not like those mules in the cartoon.

Memory Verse

"Be content with such things as ye have."—Heb. 13:5

HONEST ABE

Perhaps THE most beloved and most famous American character is Abraham Lincoln. We love him because of his wonderful achievements despite the handicap of his humble birth in an obscure place. We love him because he worked hard, educated himself, was kind, gentle, modest, friendly, and sought always to be a blessing to others.

Lincoln will always be remembered for his good humor, his wonderful eloquence, his service as President of the United States, his emancipation of the slaves, his stand against strong drink, and the sad and tragic end of his life. Another thing for which we love and remember him is his strict honesty. You remember that his nickname was "Honest Abe."

One little story will explain why he was called Honest Abe. When he was a young fellow, he clerked in a country store in Illinois. One day as he was checking over the sales and receipts of the day, he discovered he had charged a customer six cents too much for some merchandise. And so, after he closed the store, he walked two miles to the home of the customer and returned the six cents. He didn't want to wait until the customer came to the store again. He knew he would sleep better that night if he had it off his conscience. What a wonderful world this would be if we had more people like Honest Abe.

I know a storekeeper who hired a boy to work about the store. To test the boy's honesty he put some coins under a jar on a shelf, then had the boy dust off the shelf while he watched through a peephole from another room. The boy found the money and promptly turned it over to the owner, who complimented him on his honesty. That boy became a very successful businessman and was highly respected by everybody. It is said, "Honesty is the best policy." It is more than a good policy, it is a principle.

Memory Verse

"We trust we have a good conscience, in all things willing to live honestly."—Heb. 13:18

SEEING SPOTS

WHAT DO you see?" asked a primary teacher as she held up a piece of white paper about a foot square. In the center of the sheet of paper she had made a black spot with a crayon. The spot was quite small, perhaps the size of a dime. Instantly every child's hand went up. All of them thought they had the answer. "Well, what do you see?" asked the teacher. The children all answered at once, "A black spot." "Don't you see anything but a black spot?" asked the teacher. "No, ma'am," was the reply in chorus.

Then the teacher proceeded to show how they had seen the small spot, but had overlooked all the white area of the sheet of paper. Although there was two hundred times as much white area as black, they saw only the black. The lesson is very clear. A person's life may be ever so beautiful and pure, yet one little moral defect can spoil the whole.

One little fly that drops into our cup of coffee or milk spoils our drink. One little flaw in a precious gem greatly reduces its value. A great department store had a special sale of women's white gloves at a ridiculously low price. The sign on the bargain counter read, "Slightly Soiled. Price Greatly Reduced." A pastor once picked up his little grandson after Sunday school, just before the church service started. When the pastor got home after church, he discovered a black fingerprint on his white collar. That accounted for a lot of unusual smiling on the part of folk who were leaving the church.

Boys and girls, the lesson for us is that little sins can greatly detract from an otherwise good character. A little lie, a little act of dishonesty, a little fit of jealousy, or selfishness can spoil all the other fine traits in your character.

Memory Verse

"Keep . . . unspotted from the world." Jas. 1:27

VALENTINE'S DAY

ALL BOYS and girls, and many older people too, like to send and receive valentines. It is fun to pick out the ones that express our sentiments and send them to our loved ones and friends. It is even more fun to make our own valentines. Sometimes mischievous people, old and young, send valentines with ugly pictures and verses that make those who receive them feel very bad. This is not in the spirit of Valentine's Day. The real spirit of the day calls for making people happy. There is a story about Valentine's Day.

As the story goes, in the early days of Christianity, probably in the late third century, there lived a good bishop whose name was Valentine. He was greatly loved because he had a big, loving, and generous heart. He was always doing good to somebody. His great delight was to take baskets of food to the poor. He would put the baskets on their doorsteps, knock on the door, then be out of sight before the people could see who had been so kind to them. He didn't want to be thanked or praised; he just wanted to relieve distress.

In those days Christians were often persecuted and put to death just because they were Christians. Valentine was put to death, so the tradition goes, on a February 14. After he died, the baskets were no longer given to the poor. Then the people discovered who their wonderful friend had been, so they set aside February 14 as Valentine's Day.

Why is the heart a symbol of Valentine's Day? Because of the big, loving, generous heart of good Bishop Valentine. To really celebrate the day, and enter fully into its spirit, we too must have loving, generous hearts.

Memory Verse

"Love one another with a pure heart."—I Pet. 1:22

A QUEER CHRISTMAS PARTY

How would you children like to help me with the sermonette? You can help by doing some imagining. Just imagine that one of you was born on December 25. Let us say it was Bobby.

Then let us imagine that Bobby's friends decide to throw a party in his honor. So they set December 25 as the day, got a lot of candies and cakes together, decorated the house with greens, lights, and tinsel, and planned a lot of games and the exchange of gifts with each other at the party.

Now let us imagine the party is in full swing. Everybody is having a fine time, and all of a sudden there is a knock on the door. Someone answers it and who should be there but Bobby, in whose honor the party is being held. "I should like to come in and attend my party," says Bobby. "Sorry," comes the answer, "but we don't have room for you. Come some other time and maybe we'll have room for you."

Well, wouldn't that be a queer party? Just imagine, a party in Bobby's honor, but room for everybody else excepting Bobby. That just doesn't make sense, does it? Go slow in answering that question because you'll be tramping on somebody's toes. Thousands and thousands of people will have big "goings-on" in their homes at Christmas. They pretend to be celebrating Christ's birthday, but there will be no room for him. No matter how much he knocks at the door and asks for admittance, they will keep him outside. A queer party in his honor, indeed! People who don't want Christ in their hearts and homes at Christmas shouldn't celebrate Christmas. Christ should be in the center of things. Our celebration is in his honor, and our best gift should be to him.

How about you? Will there be room for Christ in your Christmas celebration?

Memory Verse
"Behold, I stand at the door, and knock."—Rev. 3:20

INDEX OF SCRIPTURES

Old Testament

INDEX OF SUBJECTS